First World War
and Army of Occupation
War Diary
France, Belgium and Germany

20 DIVISION
Divisional Troops
93 Brigade Royal Field Artillery
1 August 1915 - 31 December 1916

WO95/2106/1

The Naval & Military Press Ltd
www.nmarchive.com
Published in association with The National Archives

Published by

The Naval & Military Press Ltd

Unit 10 Ridgewood Industrial Park,

Uckfield, East Sussex,

TN22 5QE England

Tel: +44 (0) 1825 749494

www.naval-military-press.com

www.nmarchive.com

This diary has been reprinted in facsimile from the original. Any imperfections are inevitably reproduced and the quality may fall short of modern type and cartographic standards.

© **Crown Copyright**

Images reproduced by permission of The National Archives, London, England, 2015.

Contents

Document type	Place/Title	Date From	Date To
Heading	2106/1		
Heading	20th Division Divl Artillery 93rd Bde R.F.A. Aug 1915-Dec 1916 To 3 Army		
Heading	20th Division 93rd Bde. R.F.A. Vol. I Aug 15-Dec 16		
Heading	War Diary of 93rd Brigade R.F.A. from Aug 1st to 31st 1915		
War Diary	Bleu	01/08/1915	02/08/1915
War Diary	Armentieres	02/08/1915	02/08/1915
War Diary	Bleu	02/08/1915	02/08/1915
War Diary	Armentieres	03/08/1915	03/08/1915
War Diary	Bleu	03/08/1915	03/08/1915
War Diary	Armentieres	04/08/1915	04/08/1915
War Diary	Bleu	04/08/1915	04/08/1915
War Diary	Armentieres	05/08/1915	05/08/1915
War Diary	Bleu	05/08/1915	11/08/1915
War Diary	Verte Rue	12/08/1915	28/08/1915
War Diary	Rue du Haneau	28/08/1915	30/08/1915
War Diary	Fleurbaix	30/08/1915	31/08/1915
Heading	20th Divn 93rd Bde. R.F.A. Vol 2 Sept 15		
Heading	War Diary 93rd Brigade R.F.A. from September 1st to September 30th 1915		
War Diary	Fleurbaix	01/09/1915	26/09/1915
War Diary	Lavantie	27/09/1915	29/09/1915
War Diary	Rouge De Bout	30/09/1915	30/09/1915
Heading	Appendix to 93rd Bde R.F.A. War Diary for Operation Of The 25 Sept 1915		
Miscellaneous	Report On Operation directed against Enemys front from Corner Fort (N6 d.49) to Bridoux Fort (I31d.0.3) September 25 1915	25/09/1915	25/09/1915
Heading	20th Division 93rd Bde. R.F.A. Vol. 3 Oct 15		
Heading	War Diary of 93rd Brigade R.F.A. from October 1st 1915 To October 31st 1915 (Volume)		
War Diary	Rouge de Bout	01/10/1915	31/10/1915
Heading	20th Division 93rd Bde R.F.A. Vol. 4 Nov 15		
Heading	War Diary 93rd Brigade R.F.A. From Nov 1st. 1915 To November 30th 1915 (Volume)		
War Diary	Rouge de Bout	01/11/1915	23/11/1915
War Diary	Rue Biache	24/11/1915	30/11/1915
Heading	93rd Bde. R.F.A. Vol. 5 Dec		
Heading	War Diary Of 93rd Bde, R.F.A. From Dec. 1st 1915 To Dec 31st 1915 (Volume)		
War Diary	Rue Biache	01/12/1915	31/12/1915
Heading	January 1916 Missing		
Heading	War Diary 93rd Brigade R.F.A. From Feb 1st 1916 To Feb 29 1916 Volume 7		
War Diary	Le Nieppe	01/02/1916	03/02/1916
War Diary	Rubrouck	04/02/1916	12/02/1916
War Diary	Watou	13/02/1916	13/02/1916
War Diary	Elverdinghe	14/02/1916	29/02/1916

Heading	War Diary 93rd Bde R.F.A. From Mch 1st 1916 To Mch 31st 1916 Volume 6		
War Diary	Elverdinghe	01/03/1916	05/03/1916
War Diary	Poperinghe	06/03/1916	31/03/1916
Heading	War Diary Hd Qrs 93rd Bde R.F.A. 1st-30th April 1916 (Vol X)		
War Diary	Poperinghe	01/04/1916	30/04/1916
Heading	War Diary 93rd Bde R.F.A. From 1-5-16 To 31-5-16 Vol 10		
War Diary	Zeggers Cappel	01/05/1916	19/05/1916
War Diary	Ypres I.b.8.0	20/05/1916	29/05/1916
War Diary	Ypres	29/05/1916	31/05/1916
Heading	War Diary 93rd Bde R.F.A. From 1-6-16 To 30-6-16 Vol II		
War Diary	Ypres	01/06/1916	30/06/1916
War Diary	Ypres	29/06/1916	30/06/1916
Heading	20th Div. XIV Corps. Headquarters, 93rd Brigade. R.F.A. July 1916		
War Diary	Ypres	01/07/1916	31/07/1916
Heading	93rd Bde. R.F.A. 20th Div. "D" Battery. July (17.7.16-31.7.16) 1916		
War Diary	Ypres	01/07/1916	31/07/1916
Heading	93rd Bde. R.F.A. 20th Div. "A" Battery. July (7.7.16 to 31.7.16) 1916		
War Diary	Ypres	17/07/1916	31/07/1916
Heading	20th Divisional Artillery. Battery Diaries Attached 93rd Brigade R.F.A. August 1916		
Heading	War Diary Of 93rd Bde R.F.A. From 1-8-16 To 31-8-16 (Volume) XIV		
War Diary	Ypres	22/08/1916	31/08/1916
War Diary	Ypres	01/08/1916	22/08/1916
War Diary	Ypres	01/08/1916	24/08/1916
War Diary	Ypres	01/08/1916	22/08/1916
Heading	20th Divisional Artillery. 93rd Brigade R.F.A. September 1916		
Heading	War Diary 93rd Bde R.F.A. From 1st Sept 1916 To 30th Sept 1916 Vol. 14		
War Diary	Ypres	01/09/1916	06/09/1916
War Diary	Watou	06/09/1916	07/09/1916
War Diary	Oehtezeele	08/09/1916	08/09/1916
War Diary	Marthes	09/09/1916	09/09/1916
War Diary	Monchy-Cayeux	10/09/1916	10/09/1916
War Diary	Conchy-Sur-Conchy	11/09/1916	11/09/1916
War Diary	Outrebois	12/09/1916	12/09/1916
War Diary	Flesselles	13/09/1916	13/09/1916
War Diary	Bois-Des-Tailles Sur Somme	14/09/1916	18/09/1916
War Diary	Bois-Des-Tailles	19/09/1916	19/09/1916
War Diary	Guillemont	20/09/1916	30/09/1916
Heading	20th Divisional Artillery. 93rd Brigade R.F.A. October 1916		
Heading	War Diary 93rd Bde R.F.A. From 1-10-16 To 2-10-16 Vol 15		
War Diary	Guillemont	01/10/1916	01/10/1916
War Diary	Tyd Map 57CSW	02/10/1916	03/10/1916
War Diary	Guillemont	01/10/1916	01/10/1916
War Diary	Tyd Map 57CSW	04/10/1916	08/10/1916

War Diary	T.7.d. Sheet 57c.S.W.	11/10/1916	31/10/1916
Heading	20th Divisional Artillery. 93rd Brigade R.F.A. November 1916		
Heading	War Diary Of 93rd Brigade R.F.A. Nov 1st To 30th 1916 Vol 16		
War Diary	T.7.d.6.2	01/11/1916	10/11/1916
War Diary	T25a5.9.1/2	11/11/1916	11/11/1916
War Diary	T25a 591/2 (Sheet 51SW)	12/11/1916	25/11/1916
War Diary	T14c 91/2	26/11/1916	29/11/1916
Heading	20th Divisional Artillery. 93rd Brigade R.F.A. December 1916		
Heading	War Diary For Period 1st To 31st Dec 1916 Of 93rd Brigade R.F.A. Vol 17		
War Diary	T14c. 91/2 3 Sheet 57c.SW	01/12/1916	10/12/1916
War Diary	T14c A/93 B/93 T8d D/93	11/12/1916	13/12/1916
War Diary	T14c A1B/93 T8d-D/93 Sheet 57c SW.	14/12/1916	27/12/1916
War Diary	Morlancourt	28/12/1916	31/12/1916

20TH DIVISION
DIVL ARTILLERY

93RD BDE R.F.A.
AUG 1915-DEC 1916

To 3 ARMY.

121/6787

20th Division

93rd Bde: R.F.A.
vol: I

Aug 15 – Dec '16

CONFIDENTIAL.

War Diary
of
93rd Brigade R.F.A.

From Aug 1st to 31st 1915

Army Form C. 2118

WAR DIARY
or
INTELLIGENCE SUMMARY
(Erase heading not required.)

Place	Date	Hour	Summary of Events and Information	Remarks and references to Appendices
BLEU	1-8-15		Bde in Billets. Rontie work. Gym Drill or Weather Fine and hot	R.M.D
" "	2-8-15	7.30am	Parts of 3 Officers & 23 men of Bde HdQrs and 2 Officers & 18 men from each Battery marched to ARMENTIERES to be attached for instruction to "A" Group of "Dn" Arty. A/93 attached to 148" Batty 87.c. B/93" " to 95" Batty. C/93" " to 96" Batty. D/93" " to 131" Batty. Weather fine & hot.	R.M.D
ARMENTIERES		10am	Arrived	R.M.D
" "		11am	Visited Observing Station and Gun positions of these Batteries. Smyth in in senior. Weather Fine	R.M.D
BLEU	2-8-15		Remainder of Bde Routine work Drill & Weather fine	Stores
ARMENTIERES	3-8-15	10am	Visited Observing Station & Gun positions of Batteries. Weather unsettled Morning	R.M.D
			Still Very quiet	R.M.D
BLEU	3-8-15		Remainder of Bde Routine. Drill or Weather Free	Statn
ARMENTIERES	4-8-15	10am	R.H.A. & R.F.A. Engineer Officers of all parties attached to 29" Divn. A.S. when with Brigades retthing doing. Weather close unsettled.	R.M.D
BLEU	4-8-15		Remainder Bde Routine - Drill or Weather unsettled chir	R.M.D
ARMENTIERES	5-8-15	11am	All parties of the Bde attached to 29" Divn. Arty marched back to	Statn
			Billets at BLEU.	R.M.D
BLEU	5-8-15	11.30am	Arrived Weather Fine	R.M.D

Army Form C. 2118

WAR DIARY
or
INTELLIGENCE SUMMARY
(Erase heading not required.)

Instructions regarding War Diaries and Intelligence Summaries are contained in F. S. Regs., Part II. and the Staff Manual respectively. Title Pages will be prepared in manuscript.

Place	Date	Hour	Summary of Events and Information	Remarks and references to Appendices
BLEU	6-8-15		Arrived. Fortune works Co. Weather fine	R.H.D.
" "	7-8-15		do	R.H.D.
" "	8-8-15		do — Weather close unsettled	R.H.D.
" "	9-8-15		do — Fine Warm	R.H.D.
" "	10-8-15		do	R.H.D.
" "	11-8-15	8.45am	B.C. B'de M.H. Battery Commander and Am. Col. Commander visited the 4.5" B'ne R.F.A. in action asy	R.H.D.
" "			Fine Beanche 1¼ mile S.W. FLEURBAIX. Weather fine and Warm.	R.H.D.
" "	12-8-15	2pm	Marched to Billets at VERTIE RUE — CAUDESCURE Heather fine Warm	R.H.D.
VERTIE RUE	—	3pm	Arrived	
" "	13-8-15		Arrived. Bee Fortune works G. Weather Wet	R.H.D.
" "	14-8-15		do do Weather fair Showery	R.H.D.
" "	15-8-15	9am	G.O.C. & B.C's visited 38" B's R.F.A in action. Weather Wet	R.H.D.
" "		3.45pm	G.O.C. 2° Div with C.R.A. (Majn Gen R.H.Davies, C.B & Brig Gen J.HOTHAM) inspected B'es Billets, Horses, &c.	R.H.D.
" "	16-8-15		Drill Fortune Works Weather Wet	R.H.D.
" "	17-8-15		do " fine	R.H.D.
" "	18-8-15		do " fine	R.H.D.
" "	19-8-15		do " fine	R.H.D.
" "	20-8-15		do " fine	R.H.D.
" "	21-8-15		do " fine	R.H.D.
" "	22-8-15		do " fine	R.H.D.
" "	23-8-15		do " fine & hot	R.H.D.
" "	24-8-15		do " "	R.H.D.
" "	25-8-15		do " "	R.H.D.
" "	26-8-15		do " "	R.H.D.
" "	27-8-15		do " "	R.H.D.

Army Form C. 21

WAR DIARY
or
INTELLIGENCE SUMMARY.
(Erase heading not required.)

Instructions regarding War Diaries and Intelligence Summaries are contained in F. S. Regs., Part II. and the Staff Manual respectively. Title pages will be prepared in manuscript.

Place	Date	Hour	Summary of Events and Information	Remarks and references to Appendices
VERRE RUE	27.8.15	6.30am	Marched to New Billets area RUE du HAMEAU. Weather fine & hot.	9/H.S.
RUE du HAMEAU	28.8.15	10.15	Arrived. Weather fine & hot.	R.W.S.
	29.8.15		On the march fine & hot.	R.H.A
	30.8.15	6 pm	Marched to Billets at FLEURBAIX to be attached to 8th Division. Weather fine. Arrived.	R.W.S R.W.S
FLEURBAIX		9 pm		R.W.S R.W.S
	31.8.15		Batteries employed on making Gun Emplacements preparation & occupying positions at - (A/93) H34 b 1.8. (B/93) H34 b 2.9 - (C/93) H28 a 1.1. (D/93) H28 a 2.6. R.W. Bde Belgium & France (Douai) Sheet 36 N.W. Weather fine.	R.H.A R.H.A

Lt. M.M.

[signature] R.W. Bde R.F.A.

ADJUTANT 93rd BRIGADE R.F.A.

Ref. Map HAZEBROUCK 5A

8914/12

20th Divn

93rd Bde: R.F.a.
vol 2

Sept. 15.

CONFIDENTIAL.

WAR DIARY

93rd Brigade R.F.A.

From September 1st to September 30th 1915.

Army Form C. 2118.

WAR DIARY
or
INTELLIGENCE SUMMARY.
(Erase heading not required.)

Instructions regarding War Diaries and Intelligence Summaries are contained in F. S. Regs., Part II. and the Staff Manual respectively. Title pages will be prepared in manuscript.

Place	Date	Hour	Summary of Events and Information	Remarks and references to Appendices
FLEURBAIX	1-9-15		The Brigade plus "O" Battery R.H.A. forming Butler's Group controlled by Lt Col Butler (Commanding 5th Bde R.H.A.) is now for tactical purposes under the C.R.A. 8th Division and is to assist the 33rd Brigade R.F.A. in covering the Right Brigade front, roughly between BAS MAISNIL – LE BRIDOUX. In the open the Batteries are to occupy positions as follows A/93 and D/93 about 1500x SOUTHEAST of FLEURBAIX C/93 about 700x SOUTHWEST of that place. All Batteries (with the exception D/93) which takes its position occupied by 32nd Battery R.F.A.) are engaged in preparing gun emplacements prior to occupation of their positions. Weather fine. (Ref Maps Belgium & France (Bons, Sheet 36)	R.H.D.
"	2-9-15	10 a.m.	All Gun Emplacements practically completed	R.H.D.
		2 p.m.	B/93 and D/93 commenced to occupy their positions	R.H.D.
			C/93 and A/93 in position	R.H.D.
"	3-9-15	9 a.m. to	B/93 Reports on Yapres")	
		12	")	
		2.30 p.m.	C/93 ")	
		4.45 "	") Trips very much late. Weather very warm.	
		6 p.m. to		
		8.30 p.m.	A/93 and C/93 open fire on their positions. Weather unsettled	R.H.D.
"	4-9-15		All Batteries Registering Yapres. Situation quiet. Weather wet.	R.H.D.

Army Form C. 2118.

WAR DIARY
or
INTELLIGENCE SUMMARY.
(Erase heading not required.)

Instructions regarding War Diaries and Intelligence Summaries are contained in F. S. Regs., Part II and the Staff Manual respectively. Title pages will be prepared in manuscript.

Place	Date	Hour	Summary of Events and Information	Remarks and references to Appendices
FLEURBAIX	5-9-15	6.30p	All Batteries Registering Targets. Situation quiet.	R.W.D.
"	"	"	Bochum & Column arrived in Billets at about 7pm N.E. of Road Junction FORT ROMPU. SAILLY - ARMENTIERES Road. Weather unsettled	R.W.D
"	6-9-15	"	All Batteries Registering Targets. Weather fine	R.W.D.
"	7-9-15	12.30pm	All Batteries Registering Targets. Weather fine. LA BOUTILLERIE B/93 were firing — at B/93 was storming from it at the time. Situation quiet	V.R.C.D
"			Nothing to report Situation quiet Weather fine	R.W.D.
"	8-9-15		do — do — do —	R.W.D
"	9-9-15		do — do — do —	R.W.D
"	10-9-15		do — do — do —	R.W.D
"	11-9-15		do — do — do —	R.W.D
"	12-9-15		do — do — do —	R.W.D
"	13-9-15	5.15am	Enemy shelled the 20th Divn front at the same time exploding a mine in the vicinity of LA CORDONNERIE FARM. N10.b. (Trench map Sheet 36 S.W.2)	R.W.D.
"	"	5.20am	(about) received SOS message and batteries opened fire on communication trenches at N11d.	R.W.D
"	"	5.30am	(about) N16.b — 54 rounds shrapnel fired	R.W.D
"	"		(about) Ban from Group HQ to cease fire, Germans having retired	R.W.D
"			Situation quiet to remainder of day. Weather fine.	R.W.D
"	14-9-15		Situation quiet. Weather fair inclined to rain.	R.W.D.

Army Form C. 2118.

WAR DIARY
or
INTELLIGENCE SUMMARY.
(Erase heading not required.)

Instructions regarding War Diaries and Intelligence Summaries are contained in F. S. Regs., Part II. and the Staff Manual respectively. Title pages will be prepared in manuscript.

Place	Date	Hour	Summary of Events and Information	Remarks and references to Appendices
FLEURBAIX	15-9-15		Situation quiet. Weather fine.	R.W.D.
"	16-9-15		— do — — do — — do —	R.W.D.
"	17-9-15		— do — — do — — do —	R.W.D.
"	18-9-15		— do — — do — — do —	R.W.D.
"	19-9-15		— do — — do — — do —	R.W.D.
"	20-9-15	9.30am	Enemy Artillery a little more active. Shelled "O" Battery F.J.St.A. on our right, with no assistance. Aeroplane, Battery three guns out of action. No casualties to personnel. Weather fine.	R.W.D. App A.
"	21-9-15	7am	A/93 Wire cutting about the Thistle Salient. N.3.A.4.2. B.C and D/93 took advantage of any opportunities as enemies Working Detachments of Enemy Infantry Parties opposite 8th Divn. Front. Heavy Commenced in preparation for assault on the 25th Sept. Weather fine.	R.W.D.
		8am	B/93 wire cutting about Thistle Salient N.3.A.4.2.	
		10 am	During the Three periods of activity by A/93 recorded Battery 120 Rounds of Shrapnel were expended. Wire at Reacons Pr.W. 2 gaps were made in Enemy parapet 16 yards and 6 yards long and not much damaged. Range about 1900 to 1950 yards.	R.W.D.
		11 am	— do —	
		2 pm	— do —	
		4 pm	— do —	
		10 pm	Reply by Heavy Artillery. Les Mtr. Leon Vipres. Fire has been chiefly directed on LA DOUTVELLERIE opposite N.3.a. and to N.6.a. About 50 Rounds from Field Guns. 20 mm. 4.2" How. 10 from 5.9 How.	R.W.D.
		8 pm 12 midnight	No rounds from very heavy ordnance observed.	
"	22-9-15	4 am	A+B/93 bursting in support Trenches. School having Salient at N3A 4.2. C+D/93 on Support trenches N.1 7.d. 2.b.¾ to N.6.c.4.1. 32 Rounds Shrapnel per Battery (note 128 R.P.s) were fired at 4 firing pts: ½ hour. Weather fine. Tonight Moonlight night.	R.W.D.

Army Form C. 2118.

WAR DIARY
or
INTELLIGENCE SUMMARY.
(Erase heading not required.)

Instructions regarding War Diaries and Intelligence Summaries are contained in F. S. Regs., Part II. and the Staff Manual respectively. Title pages will be prepared in manuscript.

Place	Date	Hour	Summary of Events and Information	Remarks and references to Appendices
FLEURBAIX	22-9-15	9 am	A/93. Нoisi Cully Continued as Hostile Salient N37A.4.2.	A.H.S.
		11 am	— do —	
		12 noon	?	
		2 pm	120 Rounds Shrapnel Expended. Further damage to wire and parapet. Gaps slightly increased Heather Jane	
		10 pm	Reply by Enemy Artillery Arm. gun. development of any E. Co. proceeded by L LABOUTILLERIE. Shell seem to be chief direction of Enemy fire, about 60 Rnds from Field Guns 6 fm 4.2 How.	A.H.S.
—"—	23-9-15	4 am	15 fm 5.9 How. observed during the day. Still no sign of very heavy advance.	
		8 am (continuous)	As B/93 Continued Bombardment on Suffolk Trench behind Enemy Salient N37A.4.2. " " N.L.6.3.6.5 to N.6.c.4.1. 32 Rnds. Shrapnel for C & R/93 " " for battery 4 L.Bing. 2nd How. Bunger Bombgrin Argier. Battery (June 126 R.P.) Were fired	A.H.S. A.H.S. R.H.S.
		8 am	A/93 " Hois. Battery Continued as - Hostile Salient N37A.4.2.	A.H.S.
		10 am	do - do - do - do	
		12 noon	M/93 - do - do - do - do	
		2 pm		
		4.25 pm (continuous)	All Batteries (in Coynidr. With remainder of Din'l. Arty.) fired on parallel lines in the Hostile Salient. Barrage from N5.d.4.2. to N.6.c.4.4. 140 R.ds pr Field, Shrapnel (Tirée 160 R.ds).	A.H.S.
		8.2 pm	One Round lers fire on hostile gun. prosper. as above (Tirée 16 Rnds. Shrapnel)	A.H.S.
	40.	4.3 C/93 Searched during Chilak CUVANT au ROSSIGNOL in Square N.6.d. 40 Rnds. Shrapnel 20 H.E. Moon fever	A.H.S.

WAR DIARY
or
INTELLIGENCE SUMMARY
(Erase heading not required.)

Instructions regarding War Diaries and Intelligence Summaries are contained in F. S. Regs., Part II. and the Staff Manual respectively. Title Pages will be prepared in manuscript.

Place	Date	Hour	Summary of Events and Information	Remarks and references to Appendices
FLEURBAIX	23-9-15	8.30 am to 12 midnight	A & B/93"" Continued Bombardment on Support Trenches behind Enemy Salient N51.a.4.2. } 32 Rounds C & D/93"" " " " N11.d.8.6½ to N.b.c.4.1.	P.M.S.
	24-9-15	4 am	" " " "	P.M.S.
			Prepared for Battery fired 4 prs. Battery. Enemy half hour. (Since 128 R'ds) Weather very wet. Reply by heavy H.E. artillery practically nil. About 1—12 to 15 Rounds from B Bns. & Howjrs. (4.2") fell about LA BOUTILLERIE Church Trolley (23rd Infys)	P.M.S.
		4.25 am to 4.32 am	Bad B/93rd firing on Right Prange N6d. } 40 Rounds Shrapnel Expended A/93 on area between COUVANT de ROSSIGNOL & track about N6d.7.1.} for Battn (160 R'ds Total) C/93 on N.b.c.7.5. Enemy 100× Battn. fire.	P.M.S.
		8 am to 16 am	M/93 Wire Cutting about Hostile Salient N5.d.4.2. reach El-Estaples. Weather dull unsettled	P.M.S.
		10.40 am	Shoots of Hostile Battery (reported by J.O.O.) B/93rd) observed at N24 a.5.9. B/93rd Engaged. Their target results appeared very Satisfactory, fire Stopped, too misty Total time 12 mins Shrapnel fired	P.M.S.
		12 am to 2 pm	A/93 Wire cutting continued Satisfactorily. 120 R'ds Shrapnel Expended	P.M.S.
		2pm to 4 pm	B/93. Searching COURANT du ROSSIGNOL in square N6d results observed good. 40 Shrapnel 20 H.E. Expended. Weather dull unsettled.	P.M.S.
			Enemy Artillery a little more active. Fire directed at LA BOUTILLERIE, Rue Wanbot Runs fell also on CROIX MARE CMA L aol about 15 R'ds fm 4·2 How, 57 which were ""Duds"". RUE DAVID abt 1—20 fm field fm 12 pm 4·2 How	P.M.S.

1875 Wt. W593/826 1,000,000 4/15 J.B.C. & A. A.D.S.S./Forms/C. 2118.

Army Form C. 2118.

WAR DIARY
or
INTELLIGENCE SUMMARY.
(Erase heading not required.)

Instructions regarding War Diaries and Intelligence Summaries are contained in F. S. Regs., Part II. and the Staff Manual respectively. Title pages will be prepared in manuscript.

Place	Date	Hour	Summary of Events and Information	Remarks and references to Appendices
FLEURBAIX	24-9-15	7.30p to 11.30p	At B/93rd. Entered Bivouacs in Support Trenches behind Enemy Salient N.3.4.2.	A.P.S.
		4 am	" " " " N.11.T.8½.6½ to N.6.c.4.1.	
	25-9-15		36 Amm. Shapnel for Batty front & for Batty 2nd Ref Army (JNA 244 Rds) Weather Wet.	A.P.S.
			Report on Battery that carried out a Army operation shewing opening Enemy line from CORNER FORT (N.6.d.4.9.) to BRIDOUX FORT (I.31.d.0.3) Contained in appendix	
	26-9-15	9pm	The Brigade received orders thro A & 9pm "Batty's Snipe. B R.L.s to move and take up position across the XI Dm Front, C/93 and B/93 had already informed the XI Dm yesterday.	
		2-3pm	Units were carried out as follows: B/H/93 R.L.s to Rue de Paradise M.3.d.8.1. A/93 to M.1.S.6.6.4	A.P.S.
LAVANTIE		12.30p	B/93 to Rue Masselot M.12.c.8.2 Position in front & Communication Established. Weather dull unsettled.	A.P.S.
"	27-9-15		Group Composed of A/93, B/93, C/93. B/91, C/91, B/92 (Hows). and Controlled by Lt Col A.T. ANDERSON Command 93rd Bde SP HQ in "LAFLINQUE" Situation quiet. Weather very wet.	A.P.S.
"	28-9-15		SITUATION quiet. Weather Wet.	A.P.S.
"	29-9-15	9pm	Lep. LAVANTIE for ROUGE de BOUT D.C. Bde on re Group fj. Batteries having been appointed Command "CROIX BLANCHE" Group. Composed of 93rd 4th RF Battn and B/90 and C/92nd (9 How). Group to Con- fused of 61st Inf Brigade which takes from N.14.a.3.0. to N.16 c.0.3.	P.A.S.
"		3pm	arrived. Position employed in Emplacements. BHQ in Establishing Communication. Weather Wet.	A.P.S.

Army Form C. 2118

WAR DIARY
or
INTELLIGENCE SUMMARY.
(Erase heading not required.)

Instructions regarding War Diaries and Intelligence Summaries are contained in F. S. Regs., Part II. and the Staff Manual respectively. Title pages will be prepared in manuscript.

Place	Date	Hour	Summary of Events and Information	Remarks and references to Appendices
Rouge de Bout	30.9.15		All Batteries of the Bde. Registering Amm- Expense 33 Shrapnel 70 H.E. Weather unsettled	H.H.S.

F.H. Denman Lt Col.
Ay 1-93rd Bde RFA. &c.

1577 Wt. W10791/1773 500,000 1/15 D. D. & L. A.D.S.S./Forms/C. 2118.

Appendix
to
93rd Bde R.F.A. War Diary
for Operations of the 25th Sept. 1915

1

Report on Operations directed against
Enemy's front from CORNER FORT (N6 d.4.9)
to BRIDOUX FORT (I 31 d.0.3) September 25ᵗʰ 1915.

Ref. Map. Trench Map Sheets 36 N.W.3+4 & 36 S.W.1+2

1. On the night of the 23ʳᵈ/24ᵗʰ Sept. two
18 pdr Q.F. guns were placed in our front
parapet, one (in charge of 2Lt. G.M. ELLIOT A/93) at
N5 d.3.8 and one (in charge of Lt. A.T. WOOLWARD B/93)
at N5 d.9.8.

2. The final Bombardment of the Enemy position
Commenced at 4.25 am. One Battery covering
a 200ˣ section of Enemy trench immediately to
the RIGHT of the section to be assaulted firing
5 Rᵈˢ per gun in the proportion of 1 Rᵈ H.E. to
3 Rᵈˢ Shrapnel. Two Batteries participating in
a barrage on the right of position assaulted
on the Support and Communication trenches in
Square N6 d. 5 Rᵈˢ Shrapnel per gun. One
Battery was reserved for Counter-Battery work

3. The 2 Guns in the parapet fired 10 Rᵈˢ H.E. rapid
at Enemy parapet opposite them, which was
demolished at these points exposing a
communication trench to our Enfilade fire
at one point. After this both the Embrasures
fell in, due to the blast caused on

2

firing. The debris was however cleared and the guns continued at a slow rate of fire with good effect on the enemy defences. 50 R^ds H.E. and 70 Rounds H.E. were expended respectively per gun.

4. At this phase the bombardment by the Brigade lasted till 4.30 am viz 5 minutes. When the assault was delivered by the Infantry, two mines having been exploded by the Sappers at 4.29 am opposite CORNER FORT and BRIDOUX FORT the craters formed being used as rough communication trenches to the captured positions. The enemy front line was occupied with a total of two casualties only, the Infantry penetrating as far as the second and third lines in some cases, but were forced to retire to the enemy front line, portions including CORNER FORT of which were, at this time, held by our troops.

5. At 8.50 am C/93 were ordered to move to NOUVEAU MONDE to rejoin the XX Div engaged on our RIGHT in the vicinity of LAVANTIE and they evacuated their position at about 10 am.

6. At 9.20 am message received from "Butler Group" H.Q. that aviation reported parties of Infantry and Horse drawn and Motor transport were moving through ENNETIERES and LOMME towards our lines

3

evidently coming out of LILLE.

7. Our Infantry continued to hold portions of the enemy front line previously mentioned. Occasional requests being received for Artillery Support, a slow rate of fire being maintained on various portions of the front according to the requirements of the situation, varying from Section fire one minute to Battery fire one minute.

8. 11.35 a.m. (Capt. WALLACE RWR) Liaison Officer accompanying the right attack reported by telephone that the Rifle Brigade had taken 107 prisoners.

9. The situation continued much as in para: 7 until 3.57 p.m. when we received the intelligence that the Infantry had been forced to retire back to our own trenches owing to heavy Arty and Machine Gun fire, and, ~~principally~~ RWR, lack of bombs.

Through Battery Group HQ

10. At 7.30 p.m. D/93 vacated its position and marched via CROIX LES CORNEX and ROUGE de BOUT to position at M 5 a 9.7. to join the XI Div. in accordance with orders through "Battery Group HQ" received at 6.15 p.m.

11. No further events of importance occurred, the enemy not attempting any counter-attack on our position or resorting to any bombardment. The night of the 25/26 Sept.

4

passed quietly, the Brigade (less C/93 and D/93) moving out of their positions and marching to positions about LAVANTIE to re-join the XX Div. at about 4 pm to 6 pm on the 26th September.

12. The approximate total Expenditure of Ammunition for the operation was:
2388 R^{ds} Shrapnel
200 R^{ds} High Explosive
─────────
2588 Total Expenditure

R.H. Denman
LT. R.F.A.
ADJUTANT 93rd BRIGADE R.F.A.
for O.C.

121/7595.

30th Kursun

93rd Bde: R.F.A.
vol: 3

Oct 15

CONFIDENTIAL

War Diary

of

93rd Brigade R.F.A.

from October 1st 1915 to October 31st 1915

(Volume)

CROIX BLANCHE Gp/y

WAR DIARY
or
INTELLIGENCE SUMMARY
(Erase heading not required.)

Army Form C. 2118

Instructions regarding War Diaries and Intelligence Summaries are contained in F. S. Regs., Part II. and the Staff Manual respectively. Title Pages will be prepared in manuscript.

Place	Date	Hour	Summary of Events and Information	Remarks and references to Appendices
Rouge de Bout	1.10.15.	6 p.m.	Weather wet. B/93 left Colonel ANDERSON's (CROIX BLANCHE) group & went to Colonel RICARDO's group. C/92 registered with 12 rds. AX(1). All Battery wagon lines started "Horse Standing".	(1) 1st pp. A. (H.E. AX. 6.5 Hows. Shrap 1B (H.E. BX.
"	2.10.15.	6 p.m.	Weather clear & frosty. No firing.	7/B.M.
"	3.10.15.	6 p.m.	Weather wet. No firing.	7/B.M.
"	4.10.15.	6 p.m.	Weather showery. M/93, D/93 + C/92 registered. Amm: expended :- 10A. 16AX. 12 BX.	7/B.M.
"	5.10.15.	6 p.m.	Weather showery. M/93, D/93+C/93 registered. Amn exp:- 18 A. 40 AX.	7/B.M.
"	6.10.15.	7.30 p.m.	Weather clear. C/92 fired 13 BX in cooperation with an aeroplane, but result not observed owing to haze in gathering gloom of a german anti-aircraft gun. M/93 + D/93 registered. Amn Exp:- 14A 51 AX 27 BX. C/92 cooperated with an aeroplane satisfactorily.	7/B.M. (A) CROIX BLANCHE Group Appendix #> A, C, D/93, C/92-D/92.
"	7.10.15.	6.30 p.m.	Weather clean. All Batteries (except D/90) registered. C/93 + D/92 at M.G. emplacements between them.	7/B.M.
"	8.10.15.	8 p.m.	Weather clean. 9/92 + 9/93 registered. Amn Exp :- 7A. 27AX. 14 BX.	7/B.M.
"	9.10.15.	7 p.m.	Weather clean. A/93 fired 4 AX on a working party. She obtained hits.	7/B.M.
"	10.10.15.	6.30 p.m.	Weather clean. C/93 fired 5 AX at a working party. 7 ou of 8 hits. D/90+D/93 fired 18rds 1AX at 16 feet the quietness of their F.O.O.'s in answering S.O.S. messages. C/92 fired 19 DX at a M.G. emplacement. Result satisfactory.	7/B.M.
"	11.10.15.	7 a.m.	Weather clean. A/93 fired 6 A at a working party. C/93 fired 1 AX to a F.O.O. C/92 fired 4 BX who shelled in retaliation. 2 BX registering	7/B.M.
"	12.10.15.	7.30 p.m.	Weather wet. Clear after midday D/90 retaliated on enemy's trenches with 4.A. M/93 registered with 5A +1AX. C/92 retaliated on enemy line with	7/B.M.
"	13.10.15.	10.30 p.m.	21 BX. Enemy exploded a mine at 9.15 p.m. at request of infantry. A/93 fired 4A on their night lines + C/93 35 A +1AX.	7/B.M.
"	14.10.15.	8 p.m.	Weather clean. A/93 registered with 4 A+15 AX. A m/9/92 on (upon 4506 N.E.) saw flash of German gun at Horse burg as Rode.	7/B.M.
"	15.10.15.	7 a.m.	Weather misty. No firing.	7/B.M.
"	16.10.15.	7 p.m.	Weather misty. C/93 fired 2A+1AX at a working party, Ama: Col. so mum was sent to D.A.C. totally destroyed our in retreat (one testedeadly all further extend).	7/B.M.
"	17.10.15.	7.30 p.m.	Weather misty. No firing.	7/B.M.
"	18.10.15.	6.30 p.m.	Weather clean. M/93 fired 4.A to check registration. C/92 fired 23 BX in retaliation to experimental shot. The Kid change.	7/B.M.
"	19.10.15.	8 p.m.	Weather clean. M/93 fired 4 3A for calibration. C/93 retaliated with 21 A+9AX+ C/92 with 12.B. D/93 fired 1A to G of F.O.O.	7/B.M.
"	20.10.15.	7 p.m.	Weather misty. D/93 took on gun to disarm Battery position in RUE MASSELOT retaliated. German final line Trench with 38 A + unit: great success. The gun was assessed by the wheel horses directly afterwards. C/93 fired 1 AX to G of F.O.O. Major H.W. PAXTON was relieved of the command of B/93+ Lt. Col. goal G.S. Gordon + practically demolished it.	7/B.M.
"	21.10.15.	8 p.m.	Weather misty. C/92 fired 25 BX on a lorried by command of infantry suspected of harbouring M.G.s + practically demolished it.	7/B.M.
"	22.10.15.	8 p.m.	Weather clean. C/92 fired 22 (3X) + D/90 18 AX on enemy's prompt booking to the approach of infantry sent to use M.G.s on attempt to repair it.	7/B.M.
"	23.10.15.	8 p.m.	Weather clean. No firing. Work on men's dugouts started.	7/B.M.
"	24.10.15.	7 p.m.	Weather clean. M/93 registered with 10 A 17 AX. Position close to Turn of B/93 taken placed in the trenches under the command of Lt: P.C. HOYLE + H.R. GIBBONS	7/B.M. 2.15 AM
"	25.10.15.	8 p.m.	Weather misty. Position chosen for a new section of B/93 under S.M. A.T. WOOLWARD in RUE DU BOIS. No firing.	7/B.M.
"	26.10.15.	7.30 p.m.	Weather clear. Battery artillery orders sent to all batteries, Brigade in case of a return of A/93 registered with 15A+5AX. C/92 with 21A+8AX, D/93 30 with 19A, C/92	7/B.M.
"		1. H. 9 BX. D/90 finished highly lined with 14.A.		7/B.M.

Army Form C. 2118.

WAR DIARY
or
INTELLIGENCE SUMMARY.
(Erase heading not required.)

Instructions regarding War Diaries and Intelligence Summaries are contained in F. S. Regs., Part II. and the Staff Manual respectively. Title pages will be prepared in manuscript.

Place	Date	Hour	Summary of Events and Information	Remarks and references to Appendices
ROUGE DE BOUT	27.10.15	8 p.m.	Weather clean. A/93 registered with 15A & 15AX, C/93 with 11A & 4AX & fired 16 A & 4AX at a working party. D/93 registered with 19 A, D/90 with 14 A, C/92 with 6 BX & retaliated with 3 BX.	¾ 13 ft.
"	28.10.15	8 p.m.	Weather wet. A/93 fired six A at a working party, Bde. HQrs laid two telephone lines from 6th Inf. Bde. Fighting HQ Brs. to a Company Commander in the position of the front line trench held by the 11th R.B. (9th Inf. Bde.) Lines do not follow communication trenches but go straight over the top of the support trenches.	¾ 9 ft.
"	29.10.15	7 p.m.	Weather misty. D/93 retaliated with a 3 A & 15 AX, enfilading the German front line trench from the RUE MASSELOT. C/92 fired 14 BX at a M.G. emplacement. Capt. G.O.S. SMITHE appointed to the Bde. to command B/93.	¾ 8 ft.
"	30.10.15	7 p.m.	Weather clean. A/93 registered support trenches with 34 A. D/93 fired 12 A at one working party at Aefanchez. 2nd Lt. WA. MALLOWS is posted to the Bde. & attached to the Amn. Col.	¾ 13 ft.
"	31.10.15	7.30 a.m.	Weather misty, wet in afternoon. A/93 enfiladed German front line trench, by means of a forward gun, with 19 A & 11 AX.	¾ 13 ft.

NAndrew
LT. COL. R.A.
COMDG. 93rd BRIGADE. R.F.A.

93 of 13da: Rda.
tot: 4

4708/121

J. Thomson

Nov 15

Confidential

WAR DIARY
93rd Brigade R.F.A.
From Nov. 1st. 1915 To November 30th 1915.

(Volume . . . .)

Army Form C. 2118

WAR DIARY
of Croix Blanche Group.
INTELLIGENCE SUMMARY.
(Erase heading not required.)

Instructions regarding War Diaries and Intelligence Summaries are contained in F.S. Regs., Part II. and the Staff Manual respectively. Title pages will be prepared in manuscript.

Place	Date	Hour	Summary of Events and Information	Remarks and references to Appendices
Rouge de Bout	1.11.15	8 p.m.	Weather wet. A/93 & D/93 fired at a working party. Am? Exp.:- 11A.	7KIB.H.
	2.11.15	7.30 p.m.	Weather wet. A/93 fired 4.8 A at working parties.	7KIB.H.
	3.11.15	8 p.m.	Weather clear. A/93 registered with D/93 fired at a working party. C/93 fired as a counter battery to LORINGS group. Am? Exp.:- 13 A 10 AX 4.1 BX.	7KIB.H.
	4.11.15	7 p.m.	Weather clear. A/93 & A/93 retaliated. D/93 registered. Am? Exp.:- 43 A 7 AX. During absence of Brig-Gen J. HOTHAM R.A. on leave the XX Div. Arty will be commanded by Lt.Col. A.T. ANDERSON R.F.A. Croix Blanche group by Major P. SUTHER R.G.A., the 93rd Bde. R.F.A., by Capt L.R. WEBBER R.F.A. Lt. A. KINLOCH-WYLIE R.F.A. posted to the Bde. vice Lt to A/93.	7KIB.H.
	5.11.15	7 p.m.	Weather showery. D/93 fired 6A at a working party.	7KIB.H.
	6.11.15	7.30 p.m.	Weather frosty & foggy. C/93 fired 5A at a working party.	7KIB.H.
	7.11.15	7.30 p.m.	Weather cold & misty. A/93 registered with 11A. C/93 fired 19 A 4 AX at request of Infantry. In the morning whilst the mist was thick D/93 searched a road behind the German line with 15A 15 AX. Later D/93 fired 6A at request of Infantry.	7KIB.H.
	8.11.15	10 p.m.	Weather clear. C/93 fired at cross roads & at a working party. D/93 & an O.P. in a tree. C/92 at FROMELLES STATION. Am? Exp.:- 26A 4 AX 18 BX.	7KIB.H.
	9.11.15	10 p.m.	Weather clear. D/93 registered & fired at two suspected O.P.s. A/93 retaliated. Am? Exp.:- 50 A.	7KIB.H.
	10.11.15	10 p.m.	Weather showery. D/93 registered with 17 A 6 AX & fired at two suspected O.P's with 12 A.	7KIB.H.
	11.11.15	9 A.m.	Weather clear. D/93 retaliated with 28 A + C/92 with 24 BX.	7KIB.H.
	12.11.15	5 p.m.	Weather wet. No firing.	7KIB.H.
	13.11.15	7 p.m.	Weather wet. A/93 fired 7A, D/93 6 A at working parties.	7KIB.H.
	14.11.15	8 p.m.	Weather fine. A/10 Am. C/92 no longer belongs to CROIX BLANCHE group & was replaced by B/92 (How.) B/93 joined C.B. group (from RICARDO'S GP.) MAJOR J.R. RIDDELL D.S.O. R.F.A. succeeds major P. SUTNER R.G.A. in command of C.B. group. D/93 & C/93 fired at working parties. B/93 registered zero line. Am? Exp.:- 115 A 12 AX.	7KIB.H.

Army Form C. 21

WAR DIARY
of CROIX BLANCHE GROUP
INTELLIGENCE SUMMARY.
(Erase heading not required.)

Instructions regarding War Diaries and Intelligence Summaries are contained in F. S. Regs., Part II. and the Staff Manual respectively. Title pages will be prepared in manuscript.

Place	Date	Hour	Summary of Events and Information	Remarks and references to Appendices
Rouge de Bout			Weather fine	
	15.11.15	7.30AM	B/93 + B/92 registered. A/93 + C/93 fired salvoes on trench from which hostile fire on our aeroplanes appeared to come. Am. Exp:- 41A 24AX 22BX	7½B.H. Hubert
	16.11.15	7.30P.M.	Weather fine. A/93 + C/93 fired at working parties. B/93 on trench. D/93 at an O.P. + B/92 registered. Am. Exp:- 75A 8AX 22 BX.	7½B.H.
	17.11.15	8p.m.	Weather fine. C/93 + D/93 registered. Am. Exp:- 49 A 5 AX.	7½B.H.
	18.11.15	8pm	Weather fine. D/93 fired at a working party.	7½B.H.
	19.11.15	8pm	Weather fine. D/93 fired 20A 1AX at trench.	7½B.H.
	20.11.15	10 P.M.	Weather fine. A/93 moved one section to 5th Battery position + A/93 one section to A/93's position. B/93 + C/93 registered. D/93 registered for a Mobile gun in RUE MASSELOT which afterwards fired a 9p.m. B/93 fired a M.G. emplacement + a Keep out of Infantry. Am. Exp:- 122 A 30AX 11 BX.	7½B.H.
	21.11.15	9p.m.	Weather fine. A/93 completely took over 5th Bty. position received part of VIII5 Div. trench. A/93 took over A/93's position + from A/93 registered. B/93 fired at a M.G. emplacement + Keep out of Infantry. Am. Exp:- 90 A 30 BX.	7½B.H.
	22.11.15	8p.m.	Weather clear. A/93 came under Lt. Col. ANDERSON's Command again. C/93 + D/93 fired at crossroads + D/90 registered. Am. Exp:- 21A.	7½B.H.
	23.11.15	8pm	Weather foggy. All batteries fired at likely crossroads behind the German lines. Am. Exp:- 96A 1 zBX.	7½B.H.
RUE BIACHE	24.11.15	9 p.m.	Weather clear. 93rd Bde. Hd. Qrs. moved to billet in RUE BIACHE vacated by 45th Bde. Hd Qrs. RFA. All the batteries registered. Am. Exp:- 50A 45 BX.	7½B.H.
	25.11.15	8pm	Weather misty. One section of B/93 moved into 55th Battery's position after dark + one section into 3rd Battery's position. B/93, C/93 D/93 retaliated. A/93, D/93 + B/92 registered. Am. Exp:- 107 A 8A X 4BX.	7½B.H.
	26.11.15	8pm	Weather clear. B/93 took over 55th Bty. position completely + C/93 3rd Bty. New CROIX BLANCHE (RIGHT) group is now complete but under Command of VIIth Div. A/93, C/93, D/93 + B/92 registered. Am. Exp:- 74 A 5AX 9BX 11 BX.	7½B.H. O.C. B.93 + party relieved 2nd Bn. R.H.A.
			2Lt A KINLOCH – WYLIE posted to Am. Column with effect from 24th inst.	7½B.H.

WAR DIARY
of CROIX BLANCHE (or RIGHT) GROUP
INTELLIGENCE SUMMARY.

(Erase heading not required.)

Army Form C. 2118

Instructions regarding War Diaries and Intelligence Summaries are contained in F. S. Regs., Part II. and the Staff Manual respectively. Title pages will be prepared in manuscript.

Place	Date	Hour	Summary of Events and Information	Remarks and references to Appendices
RUE BLANCHE	27.11.15	8 p.m.	Weather clear. XXth Div. took over from VIIIth Div. B/93, D/93, C/90+D/90 registered. Ammo Exp:- 13A.	7LBy.
	28.11.15	9 p.m.	Weather clear. Six degrees of frost at mid-day. A/93, C/93, D/93+D/90 retaliated. B/93 registered. Ammo Exp:- 97A 33AX.	7LBy.
	29.11.15	8 p.m.	Weather wet. C/93 fired at a working party. D/93 + B/92 retaliated for shelling of left of guards Divn. Ammo Exp:- 66A 20BX.	7LBy.
	30.11.15	8 p.m.	Weather clear. C/93 fired at suspected O.P.s C/90, A/93+D/93 retaliated. Ammo Exp:- 50A 29AX.	7LBy.

H B Hitchborn
2nd Lt. R.F.A.
Orderly Officer 93rd Bde. R.F.A.

93rd Bde: R.F.A.
Vol: 5
Dec—

20.4.

CONFIDENTIAL

WAR DIARY

of

93rd Bde. R.F.A.

From Dec. 1st 1915 to Dec. 31st 1915.

(Volume   )

WAR DIARY
of Right Group (late Croix Blanche Group).
INTELLIGENCE SUMMARY.

Army Form C. 2118.

(Erase heading not required.)

Instructions regarding War Diaries and Intelligence Summaries are contained in F. S. Regs., Part II. and the Staff Manual respectively. Title pages will be prepared in manuscript.

Place	Date	Hour	Summary of Events and Information	Remarks and references to Appendices
	1.12.15	10 p.m.	Weather fine. A/93 & B/92 fired at enemy's parapet & communication trenches in conjunction with a mine exploded by our sappers. B/93 & D/93 retaliated. B/92 required. Am⁹ Exp:- 83A 20AX 9BX. All O.P.s now in lateral communication with each other.	7th Bde Hd. Qrs.
	2.12.15	8 p.m.	Weather fine. C/90 fired at a working party. A,B,C,&D/93 + D/90 retaliated. B/92 fired a suspected O.P. Am⁹ Exp :- 58 A 22AX 1B 14 BX.	7th Bde Hd. Qrs.
	3.12.15	9 a.m.	Weather wet. Too misty for observation. C/90 fired on working parties. D/93 enfiladed a salient in the enemy's lines. A/93, C/93 + D/90 retaliated. Am⁹ Exp:- 49A 15AX.	7th Bde Hd. Qrs.
Bioch	4.12.15	8:30 p.m.	Weather wet & misty. No firing done.	7th Bde Hd. Qrs. 7th Bde Hd. Qrs.
	5.12.15	9 p.m.	Weather clear. C/93, D/93 & B/92 retaliated. Am⁹ Exp.:- 71A, 20 AX, 19 BX.	
	6.12.15	1:30 p.m.	Heather clear. Wt- Wt:- A.B.C.D/93 and D/90 on N/9/92 (4·5 How.) Bombarded heavy front line from N9c41. to N9c8.2. One Batty (B/90) shelling communication trenches in rear. Section Bombarded. Much damage was caused & enemy went and parapet- and a fire suffered- in Third Trench. Parts being burried for safety. Ammⁿ Expenditure 4-1·8 pdr. Batteries 40 Rds H.E. per Batty. 1-18 pdr. (comm' Trenches) 40 Shrapnel. B/92 (4·5 How) 30 Rds H.E. Enemy Reply small, only about 30 three Gun fires from batty in our area. No operations by us. Rest heavy only fairly active. C/90 were shelled by 4·2 and 5·9. Some above 60 Rounds fired. But no hits there. position. One emplacement was unsettled but no damage done to sites- Materiel or personnel. Enemy aeroplane Co. operated. Weather dull unsettled.	R/Ht.Q. R/Ht.Q.
Rue	7.12.15	3·30 p.m.	Weather- unsettled. Enemy Shrapnel bombarded fm N9c 8.2 to N9d 2.4.2. One 18pdr- Batty- (B/90) on Comm- Trenches in rear and one fm battlefield. Very front shells and ammor damage done to- Enemy war + Parapet small. Weʳᵉ caused in one place. Batteries fired- AC & B/93 C/90. 60 Rds. H.E. pr- Batty D/90 60 R² Shrap. B/92 (4·5 How) 45 R⁸ H.E.	R/Ht.Q.
	8.12.15	12 noon		
✗	9.12.15	3 p.m.	At request of infantry a preparatn for a minor operatn. 250 R⁹ Shrapnel fired at point N16 b7 2·3·2. N16 d 4·2. N16 d 2·8. Saud wore very Diff- and more shots making it difficult to cut- but there was B/93 fired in two perods of 4· minutes each from Bty- at N16 C 4·3.	R/Ht.Q.

1577 Wt. W10791/1773 500,000 1/15 D. D. & L. A.D.S.S./Forms/C. 2118.

WAR DIARY of Right Group
INTELLIGENCE SUMMARY.

Army Form C. 2118.

(Erase heading not required.)

Place	Date	Hour	Summary of Events and Information	Remarks and references to Appendices
The BIACHE	10.12.15	2.30p	Weather dull & unsettled. Two (2) New Batteries of 4.5" How. Battered enemy parapet where it crosses the RIVER LAIES. N.8.d.9.1. With object of looking up the fire at that point - 50 R²HE.	RHA
	11.12.15		Were opened on all about the parapet. No much knocked about. The debris falling in to the river. B/93 continued to cut-wire a front line and trenches in parapet. Wire made at point N.10.d.4.9. D/90 also cut-wire at N.9.c.1.2 and N.9.c.8.2. 100 R² Shrapnel Longshort. Hostile Artillery.Some shells were fired at odd times from (?) to the (?) the Tramway dump N.22.c.8.0. A/93 C/93 D/93 and D/90. 20 R² Shrapnel per Batty. D/93 and D/90.	RHA
			Nervous Wire Cutty speaking and further came were Cent M. N.10 d 33.75 and N.9 c 2.12. 100 R²	
			Practiced at dawn finish.	
	12.12.15	9 am 3.20p	Weather dull & Conglig. No Hostile Arty. Heavy shelled D/93 about 140 Rounds. 5.9 and 4.2 Gen Shells falling in and about the Battery. No damage done.	RHA
	13.12.15	2p	Hostile Guns: Wotter Shell + mot.	RHA
	14.12.15 15.12.15	— 2pm	Weather dull, Heavy Snow. Enemy Defences at 1st and H.O Y 9 N (N 22 d 1.6) bombarded Increasing Barrage point-of-aim fell in and about the house Battn taking position A.C.D/93.	RHA RHA
			C/90 60 R² S D.C.5. p.6 Batty, B/92 (4.5" How) 30 R² HE.	RHA
	16.12.15	2.30am	Stand-to! No hostile. An organised raid was made by our infantry on enemy front by the River Lanes but the Battn discovered about coff for an attempted to our own trenches without coming upon a coolest with any fire.	RHA

Army Form C. 2118.

WAR DIARY of Right Group
INTELLIGENCE SUMMARY.
(Erase heading not required.)

Instructions regarding War Diaries and Intelligence Summaries are contained in F.S. Regs., Part II. and the Staff Manual respectively. Title pages will be prepared in manuscript.

Place	Date	Hour	Summary of Events and Information	Remarks and references to Appendices
Rue Biache	17.12.15	9 p.m.	Weather misty. B.C. + D/93, C + D/90, C + B/92 + B/92 fired at likely cross roads + communication trenches. Amn. Exp.:— 2.5 A 88 AX 12 BX.	92/BN.
	18.12.15	9 p.m.	Weather misty. Nothing done.	7K BN.
	19.12.15	7 p.m.	Weather fine. C+D/93 + C/90 fired at a house suspected of being a Battalion HQrs. at N22d86 (Trench Map Sheet 36 SWA). At 11.15 a.m. C/90 received 52 German S.Q's. No casualties, the only thing hit being a disused gun pit. At 2.45 p.m. 70 more S.Q's were fired on to C/90. Again no casualties. A/93 retaliated with 4 salvoes into Fromelles + 2 salvoes at F.M.E. de la Mariague. Amn. Exp.:— 36 A 66 AX	7K BN.
	20.12.15	2.30 p.m.	33 BX. Weather misty. B/93 cut wire at N10d I + E 7½ where the trenches are about 75 yds. apart. The guns did not steady until after the first 50 rounds. A breach about 8 feet wide was made in the parapet. A gap of about 12 ft. on wire the wire was made. A total breach of about 30 feet. 150 rounds shrapnel were used.	7K BN.
		3.30 p.m.	C/90 cut wire, apparently satisfactorily. Fuller report awaited from Infantry. 75 rounds shrapnel, 25 H.E. used. Corpl. A.T. ANDERSON wounded in hand at CORDONNERIE F.M.E. on way to trenches to observe fire.	91 BN. / 7K BN.
	21.12.15	12 noon	Weather extra misty. B/93 cut wire in one place with 12 A + B1 AX. C/90 cut knee place with 100 A. Capt. G.O. SMYTHE (B/93) wounded in upper arm while observing in trenches.	7K BN.
		Later	A/93 + D/93 retaliated on enemy with 12 A + B1 AX, capt. S 74 A 44 A.	
	22.12.15	7 p.m.	Weather wet + misty. A/93 checked lines with 5 A 44 A.	7K BN.
	23.12.16	2.30 p.m.	Weather misty. C/90 cut wire in one place with 85 A + 23 AX. Result difficult to observe. A.B.C. + D/93 retaliated on enemy with 66 A 157 AX. Capt. G.O. SMYTHE went to England.	7K BN.
	24.12.15	9 A.M.	Weather wet. A/93 + D/93 retaliated on enemy 9 A + 6 AX.	7K BN.
	25.12.15	2.30 p.m.	Weather fine. B/93 fired at a suspected enemy O.P., obtaining 6 direct hits, + also retaliated on enemy 1 A + 1 AX. Amn. Exp.:— 12 A 21 AX.	7K BN.
	26.12.15	7-8.30 a.m. 2 p.m.	Weather fine. All batteries fired along the FROMELLES tramway line with 8 H.E. + 8 shrapnel. D/93 report line considerably damaged. All batteries fired 16 H.E. 12 shrapnel (B)/92 24 BX) at LES CLOCHERS + houses in vicinity. During the day C/93 + C/90 retaliated at the request of the infantry. Total Amn. Exp. to day:— 3 HE 7 A 146 AX 50 BX. (3/92, 16 BX)	7K BN.
	27.12.15	11 a.m.	Weather fine. At 11 a.m. 7 p.m. all batteries opened on enemy trenches at FME DELAFORTE. Between 4.30 + 9.50 p.m. all btys. fired six salvoes along enemy's 2nd line, ADDSS. Amn. Exp. 76 A 240 AX 64 BX.	7K BN.

Army Form C. 2118

WAR DIARY
of Right Group
INTELLIGENCE SUMMARY
(Erase heading not required.)

Instructions regarding War Diaries and Intelligence Summaries are contained in F. S. Regs., Part II. and the Staff Manual respectively. Title Pages will be prepared in manuscript.

Place	Date	Hour	Summary of Events and Information	Remarks and references to Appendices
Rue Biache	28.12.15	9.30A.M. 12 p.m.	All Batteries in the group bombarded Pioneer depot at the FME. DU HOYON. C/90 L3/93, B/72, C/90 r D/90 also retaliated during the day. Arti Rep:- 158A 287 AX 34 BX. Weather wet.	7x B/H.
	29.12.15	10 a.m.	All batteries fired at fortified houses in vicinity of LES CLOCHERS. Arti Rep:- 153A 145 AX 76 BX. Weather wet.	7x B/H.
	30.12.15	12 noon 12.15pm	Weather fine. All batteries fired on enemy works round FME DE LAPORTE (N15A7.6 – N15 63.8)(Sheet 36 S.W.) Arti Rep:- 62 A 248 AX 50 BX.	7x B/H.
	31.12.15	9pm	Weather misty. All Btys.fired at BRASSERIE (PM E. DE LA FAVEILLE) in FROMELLES. Enfilade gun fired 15 rds.shrapnel at intervals between 2.30 & 6.30 A.M. along enemy parapets support trenches C/90 retaliated. Arti Rep:- 158A 210 AX 66 BX.	7x B/H.

Wandering Holmes
Cmdt 7 Gp Rgd

January 1916

Missing

20/93
93RFA Vol 7

CONFIDENTIAL

War Diary
93rd Brigade R.F.A.
From Feb 1st 1916 to Feb 29, 1916

Volume

WAR DIARY of 93rd Bde. R.F.A.
or
INTELLIGENCE SUMMARY

Army Form C. 2118.

Instructions regarding War Diaries and Intelligence Summaries are contained in F.S. Regs., Part II. and the Staff Manual respectively. Title pages will be prepared in manuscript.

Place	Date	Hour	Summary of Events and Information	Remarks and references to Appendices
LENEPPE	1.2.16	6 p.m.	Weather dull. Drill & fatigues for Batteries.	93.Bde.
"	2.2.16	10 A.M.	XX'S Divl. Art. marched past SIR HERBERT PLUMER, G.O.C. 2nd ARMY, in drill order at NORDPEENE.	93.Bde.
"	3.2.16	6 p.m.	" Drill & fatigues for Batteries.	93.Bde.
RUBROUCK	4.2.16	noon	wet. Brigade marched to RUBROUCK, arriving at 11 A.M. Brigade was incorporated in 14th Corps, which consists of GUARDS, VIth & XXth Divns.	93.Bde.
"	5.2.16	6 p.m.	Weather fine. Drill & fatigues for Batteries.	93.Bde.
"	6.2.16	6 p.m.	" " LT.COL. A.T. ANDERSON relinquished command of the Bde. on the return of GEN. J. HOTHAM resumed Command of the Bde.	93.Bde.
"	7.2.16	6 p.m.	Weather wet. Drill & fatigues for Batteries.	93.Bde. 93.Bde.
"	8.2.16	6 p.m.	" fine "	93.Bde.
"	9.2.16	6 p.m.	" " "	93.Bde.
"	10.2.16	6 p.m.	" " A/93, D/93 + C/93 sent a section each to WATOU.	93.Bde.
"	11.2.16	9 p.m.	" " These sections went into action at ELVERDINGHE relieving sections of A/48, C/48 + B/48 respectively.	93.Bde.
"	12.2.16	6 p.m.	" " One gun of C/93 received a direct hit. No one was near the gun so the only damage was to materiel. The shield & sights being smashed.	93.Bde.
"	13.2.16	6 p.m.	Weather wet. Drill & fatigues for Batteries. " Bde. H.Q. & remaining sections of A, C & D/93 marched to WATOU, just outside the borders of BELGIUM. To final time the Bde. has been in BELGIUM. B/93 sent one gun up to replace damaged one of C/93.	93.Bde. 93.Bde.
WATOU				
ELVERDINGHE	14.2.16	2 p.m.	Weather fine. LT.COL. A.T. ANDERSON took over command of the LEFT GROUP from LT.COL. BROWELL of 48 F.A. Bde. Remaining sections of A, C + D/93 came into action. AnoCol. marched from RUBROUCK to LES new quarters 2 miles W. of ELVERDINGHE. CAPT. C.L. KNIVETT posted to B/93 to command.	93.Bde.
"	15.2.16	6 p.m.	Weather fine. Windstrong. B/93 marched from RUBROUCK to Bde. wagon lines 1½ miles W. of POPERINGHE	93.Bde.
"	6.2.16	6 p.m.	Weather fine. Remaining batteries registered.	93.Bde.
"	7.2.16	6 p.m.	" Was very strong. Batteries one retaliated.	93.Bde.
"	18.2.16	6 p.m.	" wet. Batteries registered.	93.Bde.

WAR DIARY
of 9th Bde R.G.A.
INTELLIGENCE SUMMARY

Ref. Map. Boesinghe
2nd Army Sheet 1.

Army Form C. 2118

Place	Date	Hour	Summary of Events and Information	Remarks and references to Appendices
ELVERDINGHE	19-2-16	10 pm	Weather misty. The LEFT GROUP mentioned under 14th inst. consists of A.C. & D/93, A.B. & C/91, 9C/92. B/91 has two guns on the other side of the canal, one in a culvert like the other, two in The other two guns are placed in emplacements during the day but wander up & down the roads firing at night. [Germans attacked a listening post F34c93] S.O.S message received at 5pm. 10 min rapid fire. A/93 fired 155 rds. C/93 229 rds. D/93 451 rds, A/91 150 rds, C/92 197 rds. During day 4000 rds had in all, owing to use of our bombing posts F34c93, A/91 150rds, in morning	9/1/16
"	20-2-16	7pm	Weather dull. Bombardment of enemy tr[e]nches as yesterday. Enemy substituted heavily that	9/1/16
"	21-2-16	4pm	Weather fine. Bombardment of enemy front trenches as yesterday. Snipers Obs. shelled. Obsn direct hits	9/1/16
"	22-2-16	8pm	on house but no damage to personnel. Enemy aeroplane ranged on their S9 battery	9/1/16
"	23-2-16	4pm	Weather dull & cold. B/93 came into action & registered. Battery tried to cut wire at Hooge rd. & Right bad for observation	9/1/16
"	24-2-16	9pm	Were seemingly successful. Snow fell. Battery carried out small bombardment & registered point F34a 33 Weather cold. Snow late. Totally destroyed. Snow 1 foot. B/91 gun in a culvert on the E side of the Canal received a direct hit from a 5.9 gun. Must now be removed. No damage to others. Battery registered & rehabilitated a new aerial torpedo. One section of D/92 joined K group for expending	9/1/16
"	25-2-16	4pm	Snow. Battery registered & rehabilitated. Night Salvoes fired.	9/1/16
"	26-2-16	10pm	" " " 3 men wounded D/93	9/1/16
"	27-2-16	6pm	Weather fine " " " C/93 gun returned from Ordnance.	9/1/16
"	28-2-16	8pm	Weather wet " " "	9/1/16
"	29-2-16	8pm	– do – No operations by us. Enemy Arty - fairly quiet.	9/1/16

J.F.N. Kennion Capt. 9th RGA
Aug 9-93 2nd in Command RFA Bde

20/
93 RFA
Vol 6
8

Confidential
War Diary
93rd Bde R.F.A.
From Mch 1st 1916 to Mch 31st 1916

Volume.

Army Form C. 2118

WAR DIARY
or
INTELLIGENCE SUMMARY

(Erase heading not required.)

Ry Map. DOESINGHE
2nd Army Sheet 1

Instructions regarding War Diaries and Intelligence Summaries are contained in F. S. Regs., Part II. and the Staff Manual respectively. Title Pages will be prepared in manuscript.

Place	Date	Hour	Summary of Events and Information	Remarks and references to Appendices
ELVERDINGHE	1-3-16	10.30am	Weather fine but dull. Bombardment of our old trench F31 carried out by O/q> (3mm) and Conynichi with the French batty on our left-	[initials]
		3pm	Stokkur Mor. O/q1 and O/q> (2mm) Bombardment Enemy front line from C14262 to C14 to a.i. No lift from enemy -	[initials]
		9pm	Weather fine. Enemy arty fairly active all day	[initials]

Army Form C. 2118.

WAR DIARY
or
INTELLIGENCE SUMMARY.
(Erase heading not required.)

Ref. Map BOESINGHE
2nd Army Sheet 1

Place	Date	Hour	Summary of Events and Information	Remarks and references to Appendices
ELVERDINGHE	2.3.16	4.32 am and 4.47 am	Bursts of fire by A/93, C/93 & D/93 on enemy line Suppys. Communications in rear C.7.d.1.6. & C.7.d.8.6. Saps, Work-parties & ration parties. This was a demonstration in conjunction with an Infantry feint on the left of our Brigade in this Division sector. The "Boche" shewed little fight and our shrapnel [?] any apparent retaliation.	A/93.D.
	3.3.16	4pm	Weather fine but dull. Enemy Artillery fairly active during the day. No [?] by us.	A/93.
		6pm	Weather dull & Misty. Enemy Artillery being active. No calls from Infantry for retaliation where necessary. Answer [?] [?] [?] [?]	A/93.B.
	4.3.16	2pm 3.30pm 4.45pm	Bursts of fire by A/93, C/93, D/93, on our old trenches F30, F31, F34. The Heavies and the French co-operated. Enemy artillery replied vigorously to the burst at 3.10 p.m. 2/Lt G.C. CLARK and 2/Lt T.R BROWN slightly wounded in A/93. O.P.	G.712.
	5.3.16	12.35pm 2.15pm 4.15pm	Bursts of fire by A/93, C/93, D/93 on our old trenches F 30, 31, 34. The Heavies and the French co-operated. Enemy did not reply heavily.	93.
POPERINGHE	6.3.16	3pm	Weather fine. Ptes. 2nd RI Came into action. Command 7 Lt. Col. being handed over to O.C. 91st Bde R.F.A. Lt-Col. A.T. ANDERSON O.C. 93rd Bde R.F.A having been appointed to Command the Artillery of the 64th Div in England.	A/93.D.
"	7.3.16 16 14.3.16		Pte take over by Ptes. 2nd Q.I.D. Battery Operation reported on being 7 O.C. Left b/p.	A/93.
"	15.3.16		Major A.H.D. Went from 'N' Battery R.H.A. posted to Command 93rd Bde R.F.A vice Lt.Col A.T. ANDERSON.	P.M.R
"	16.3.16	6pm	Weather fine. 2 Killed 3 wounded D/93. 1 wounded C/93. (men) at ELVERDINGHE	A/93.D.

Army Form C. 2118.

WAR DIARY
or
INTELLIGENCE SUMMARY.
(Erase heading not required.)

Place	Date	Hour	Summary of Events and Information	Remarks and references to Appendices
POPERINGHE	17.3.16		Weather unsettled 1 N.C.O. killed D/93 at ELVERDINGHE	A.A.H.
"	18.3.16		" Capt. L.M. NEBBER Commanding D/93 Wounded at ELVERDINGHE	A.A.I.
"	19.3.16		"	A.A.S.
"	20.3.16		" Routine work	
"	21.3.16		" " "	
"	22.3.16		" " "	
"	23.3.16		" Wet "	A.A.D.
"	24.3.16		" " "	
"	25.3.16		" " "	
"	26.3.16		" " "	A.A.R.
"	27.3.16		Weather fine "	
"	28.3.16		" " "	
"	29.3.16		" " "	
"	30.3.16		" " "	
"	31.3.16		" " "	

R.K. Newman Capt. RFA.
Adj: 93rd Bde RFA
fr O.C.

93" Vol 9

Note: This Bde HQrs was not actually in the line, and its batteries were under Left Arty Group Commander 20th Divl Arty in the period

20 Divs

Confidential

War Diary

H.Q. 93rd Bde R.F.A.

1st — 30th April 1916

(Vol X)

WAR DIARY
or
INTELLIGENCE SUMMARY
(Erase heading not required.)

Army Form C. 2118

Place	Date	Hour	Summary of Events and Information	Remarks and references to Appendices
POPERINGHE	1-4-16 to 19-4-16		Weather unsettled. Batteries speak of shoots in left group "20" to arty. summary.	Pl. 93.
"	"	5 pm	Weather mild & cold. One section of the 7 Amy Brothers at ELVERDINGHE	Pl. 3 to 5.
"	"		returned to 6" Div. 258/93 at Pl. 93.	
"	20-4-16	"	Weather wet. 2nd section of 75/93 and Pl. 93 and the 2nd R.G. of Pl.93. relieved by 6" Hi arty.	Pl. 9 to	
"			The Battn. to R. Col. D.H.R. branched to West above ZEGGERS CAPPEL with	
"			The S. Coyps of Pl. 93 which remained on order and was attached to 6" Hi arty	Pl. 9 to.
"			The Division again rest, but also arty of G.H.Q. and XIV Corps reserve	Pl. 9 to.
21-4-16	9 am		Weather fog rest dull. All units with units in Juliet	Pl. 9 to.
"	22-4-16	9 -	Fine. All amm's. continue work & training	Pl. 9 to. Pl. 9 to.
"	23-4-16	9 -	" " " " " " " "	Pl. 9 to.
"	24-4-16	9 -	" am Pl. " " " " " "	Pl. 9 to.
"	25-4-16 to	9 am	" " " " " " " "	Pl. 9 to.
"	30-4-16	9 am	" " " " " " " "	Pl. 9 to.
"	"	9.30 pm	Pl. 93 arrives from ELVERDINGHE having been relieved by 75/9 !	Pl. 9 to.

P.H. Denman Capt. for O.C.
ADJUTANT 18TH BRIGADE R.F.A.

93. RFA
Vol. 10

Confidential

War Diary

93rd Bde R.F.A.

(20)

From 1-5-16

To 31-5-16

Army Form C. 2118

WAR DIARY
or
INTELLIGENCE SUMMARY
(Erase heading not required.)

Instructions regarding War Diaries and Intelligence Summaries are contained in F.S. Regs., Part II and the Staff Manual respectively. Title Pages will be prepared in manuscript.

Place	Date	Hour	Summary of Events and Information	Remarks and references to Appendices
ZEGGERS CAPPEL	1-5-16	9.am	Weather fine. All Batteries & A.C. re-drilling on time work etc.	R/A
	2-5-16	"	" " " " " "	R/A
	3-5-16	"	" " " " " "	R/A
	4-5-16	"	Unsettled " " " " "	R/A
	5-5-16	"	Wet " " " " "	R/A
	6-5-16	"	Wet " " " " "	R/A
	7-5-16	"	Unsettled " " " " "	R/A
	8-5-16	11.30am	Unsettled. The Brigade (with remainder of 20th Div Arty) inspected on the march by G.O.C.	R/A
	9-5-16	9 am	2nd Army (Divisional parade).	R/A
			Weather Wet - All units drill routine work R.	Em.
	10-5-16	9 am	Weather fine all Batteries & A.C. Drilling & routine work etc.	Em.
	11-5-16	All am snow	D/93, 18 Pdr Battery exchanged billets with A/92 (How) Battery.	Em.
	12-5-16	12 noon	D/93 changed name to C/92 & came under command of O.C. 92nd Bde & D/92 (How)	2nd Ret. O.B. B16 & Q.H.R.
			Battery changed name to D/93 & came under command of O.C. 93rd Bde weather fine.	2nd 20th Div Arty 6236.
	12-5-16	6 am.	93rd Bde Amm Col. Came under command of O.C. 20th Div. Amm. Col. During day	Ret O.B. B18 Q.H.R.
			Remainder of units drilling routine work weather fine.	20th Div Arty 5234.
	13-5-16		20th Div'l Arty Horse Show - weather fine.	Em.
	14-5-16	9 am	Weather dull. All Batteries redrilling and routine work etc.	Em.
	15-5-16	10 a.m.	Battery Commanders & one subaltern per Battery proceed in motor-buses to VLAMERTINGE in connection with relief between 20th Div'l Arty & Guards Div'l Arty.	Ret 20th Div Arty 0.343/1 & supply.
	16-5-16	10 am	Weather fine. All Batteries Routine & Drill.	R/A
	17-5-16	"	" " " " " "	R/A
	18-5-16	"	" " " " " "	R/A
	19-5-16	"	" " " " " "	R/A

WAR DIARY or INTELLIGENCE SUMMARY

Army Form C. 2118

(Erase heading not required.)

Left Group 20th Div Arty
Ref. Map Sheet 28 St Julien

Place	Date	Hour	Summary of Events and Information	Remarks and references to Appendices
YPRES I.16.8a.	20.5.16	4 p.m.	Bttn took over sheve of line (from I 5 b 9 3 to C 22 L 7 0) from Left Group. Guns to 2nd A.G. Group composed as follows (from Right to Left) A/93, C/90, 6 in 9/93, B/90, D/93 and 2.6 in 9/93, C/93, D/93 Howr. Valley in Reserve to all Group front. 1 Gun C/93 in reserve at Vlam line. Received information from O.C. D/90 that enemy were making a bombing attack against A.b. near I 5 b	9/90
		11.30 p.m.	following. Bullets fired on enemy line - A/93 shot 70 Rds C/93 shot 100 Rds D/93 (How) 15 H.E. enemy did not get ... on trenches. We ... about 6 casualties. Re left 1 Officer + 1 N.C.O. in no man's land. Fresh ... came fire	9/93
	21.5.16	9 p.m.	Quiet by ... at 11.40 p.m. Infantry having repulsed all genads. Later ... Khaki Mo. ... 11.45 pm ... Weather fine. a fairly quiet day. Enemy shelled Yarra bomb's on our front. Otherwise retaliated	9/93 9/90
	22.5.16	"	" " " "	
	23.5.16	"	During the night D/93 firing on enemy parties. D/93 (How) fired on enemy Sap ... Close to ARGYLE Farm with same effect (36 R.?.W). Enemy A.G. fairly active replied to our fire by ... weather fine.	9/90
	24.5.16	"	" " " front close of aircraft activity by both sides. Weather unsettled very little activity on either side.	2 w.o.
	25.5.16	7.30 a.m.	Enemy working party at I 6 6 9.8 reported by infantry successfully engaged by C/90. + dispersed	2 w.o.
		4 p.m.	Much aerial activity by both sides. A quiet day - weather generally unsettled	2 w.o.
	26.5.16	8 p.m.	Weather Fine. a quiet day with no failure of interest to report.	R/P
	27.5.16	8 p.m.	Intermittent shelling of YPRES throughout the day + great deal of airplane activity. We retaliated Artillery Weather fine.	R/P R/P
	28.5.16	8 p.m.	" Enemy shelled roads in the neighbourhood lightly.	R/P R/P
	29.5.16	7.30 a.m.	" Enemy A.G. fairly active during the day also much aerofare activity on both sides. Enemy aero last August 22/29.	R/P
			An enemy plane afterwards ... descent in ... behind his own line apparently hit by our A.A. Guns	9/90

1875 Wt. W593/826 1,000,000 4/15 J.B.C.&A. A.D.S.S./Forms/C.2118.

Army Form C. 2118.

WAR DIARY
or
INTELLIGENCE SUMMARY.
(Erase heading not required.)

Instructions regarding War Diaries and Intelligence Summaries are contained in F. S. Regs., Part II. and the Staff Manual respectively. Title pages will be prepared in manuscript.

Place	Date	Hour	Summary of Events and Information	Remarks and references to Appendices
YPRES	29-5-16	7.30p	During day one of our planes engaged a hostile machine and the apparently shot down by it descending in our lines near the LILLE GATE. Later of course no trace known	P.M.
"	30-5-16	7p	Weather fine. A very quiet day. With no facture of interest to report.	S.P.D.
"	31-5-16	7p	Weather fine. Enemy hty fairly active this morning shelled No Sparks & again no retaliation by us.	P.M.

R.H. Denman
Capt for OC
ADJUTANT 33rd BRIGADE R.F.A.
R.F.A.

93. R.F.A.
vol II
June

~~XI~~

Confidential

War Diary.

93rd Bde R.F.A

From 1-6-16

To 30-6-16.

Army Form C. 2118.

WAR DIARY
or
INTELLIGENCE SUMMARY.
(Erase heading not required.)

Instructions regarding War Diaries and Intelligence Summaries are contained in F. S. Regs., Part II. and the Staff Manual respectively. Title pages will be prepared in manuscript.

Place	Date	Hour	Summary of Events and Information	Remarks and references to Appendices
YPRES	1.6.16.		Some aerial activity, otherwise a quiet day. 2 men of A/20 RFA wounded slightly. Weather fine.	RE
"	2.6.16.	8.30 a.m	Weather fine. A bombardment commenced on our right & the front held by the Canadians and on a portion of the XX Division front extending from RAILWAY WOOD to ZWARTELEEN. It was very violent and most intense about Hill 62 and SANCTUARY WOOD. Right Group barraged RAILWAY WOOD to BELLEWAARDE CRICK. Two hostile batteries in action enfilading the HOOGE Salient were engaged by this Group with some success. In the afternoon the Germans were reported to have taken SANCTUARY WOOD and ARMAGH WOOD, and the Canadians to be holding the line : East end of MAPLE COPSE to RUDKIN HOUSE.	RE
"	3.6.16.		A fairly quiet day. News was received at 10.30 a.m. that we had recaptured 55-60, and that the Germans were retiring through SANCTUARY WOOD.	RE
"	4.6.16.		A quiet day until 8 p.m. A heavy bombardment then started on SANCTUARY WOOD, and YPRES was heavily shelled. News was received later that the Germans had attacked and had been repulsed. Mr. T. HARVIE severely wounded in the evening.	RE
"	5.6.16.		Weather showery. Very quiet day all day.	RE
"	6.6.16.	2 a.m.	Heavy bombardment at the night 1.15 p.m. a bombardment commenced on A5-A8 RAILWAY WOOD, ZOUAVE WOOD and HOOGE. At 2.45 p.m. S.O.S. A5 was received. At the same time the enemy	RE

Army Form C. 2118.

WAR DIARY
or
INTELLIGENCE SUMMARY.
(Erase heading not required.)

Instructions regarding War Diaries and Intelligence Summaries are contained in F.S. Regs., Part II. and the Staff Manual respectively. Title pages will be prepared in manuscript.

Place	Date	Hour	Summary of Events and Information	Remarks and references to Appendices
YPRES	6.6.16		Sprang two mines at RAILWAY WOOD, and put up a smoke barrage from A2-176. It was accompanied later that night by 2 small patrols approached A6. The action of the enemy on this Corps front appeared to be a demonstration to help the attack further South. 2 men of A/93 were wounded, and 3 men killed and 4 men wounded of D/93, also one howitzer of D/93 was put out of action. 2 men of [?]	[initials]
	7.6.16		A fairly quiet day. Enemy shelled x-roads lightly, and YPRES dist desultorily.	[initials]
	8.6.16		Desultory shelling of YPRES and neighbourhood throughout day. POTIJZE WOOD shelled with 5.9's and 4.2's. Otherwise normal.	[initials]
	9.6.16		A6,7,8, B9,10,11 lightly shelled with 4.2's and 77mm during day. Otherwise fairly quiet.	[initials]
YPRES	10.6.16		Bg. B10, B11 lightly shelled with 4.2's and 77 mm during day. 40 behind Bg.B10 Support trenches A. POTIJZE WOOD and support trenches A also received some 4.2 cm & 77 mm. Between 4 pm & 5 pm the DEAD End & Group HQrs by Bridge 1A were shelled with 5.9 cm & 4.2 cm. fairly heavily. On the whole enemy artillery fairly active. Weather fine.	2uo
	11-6-16		A5, A4, A8 received some 4.2 cm & 77 mm. A quiet day on the whole. The DEAD END shelled at odd intervals during the day. Weather unsettled	2uo 2uo 2uo
	12-6-16		Weather dull, wet. Relying smoke noted from L. to L. Lily. No. 4/H- hostile battery opposite our front another intermittent fire during the afternoon & began to assist operation by Canadian Corps on our front.	[initials]

T2134. Wt. W708-776. 500000. 4/15. Sir J. C. & S.

WAR DIARY or INTELLIGENCE SUMMARY

Army Form C. 2118.

Place	Date	Hour	Summary of Events and Information	Remarks and references to Appendices
YPRES	13.6.16	1.30 am	In order to annoy the Canadian Corps on our right in their attack about HILL 60 & HOOGE WOOD demonstrations were carried out about the MOUND I.5.b. and the NIEPPE Salient C.29.a.6.0. At the former place a Rifle barrage and 6 H.E. projects from the Enemy front. with breeze, aff. which a Stokes/Catapult action the MOUND to gain information by return to our lines safely. (with Weight - 1 man Anxiety Neurosis). 3.10 pm Battn bombarded NIEPPE Salient and 3-10 pm Bastion Road Pits nr. C.4.5. Hun Patrol the MOUND. All portions of the 93rd Bde were engaged in this operation. The MOUND was replied as ANTHYEL Enemy wire straight/heavily damaged. 2" T.M.s also operated against MOUND Work Front sheet. The attitude / the Enemy M.G. fire / Henwing & after the return of our Infantry to be on our line a/c 2.10 am the remainder of the Morning passed quietly. Relate to the situation Enemy arty fairly active throughout the day approximate total - 6/c any time Enemy - 150 grenades. The Meutin Hill very high	[signature]
YPRES	14.6.16 1.15pm		An exceptionally quiet day The DEAD END received a few s.a.a. during the afternoon	2uo
	6 pm		practically no Artillery activity. weather much rain	2uo
YPRES	15.6.16 6 pm		Another quiet day, practically no activity. Weather unsettled	2uo
YPRES	16.6.16 9.10 pm		Very quiet during morning. During afternoon Enemy Artillery fairly active on our front line support trenches also shelled. Weather fine generally	2uo
			YPRES, YPRES Salient, Polijze Wood	2uo

Army Form C. 2118.

WAR DIARY
or
INTELLIGENCE SUMMARY.
(Erase heading not required.)

Instructions regarding War Diaries and Intelligence Summaries are contained in F. S. Regs., Part II. and the Staff Manual respectively. Title pages will be prepared in manuscript.

Place	Date	Hour	Summary of Events and Information	Remarks and references to Appendices
YPRES	16-6-16	11.45 pm	A heavy bombardment heard on our right — at first could not get news except that it was on left of Division on our Right.	2uo
YPRES	17-6-16	12.05 am	S.O.S. H-B came thro' from Right Group — this was shortly afterwards cancelled and news came thro' that there was an enemy gas attack on the left of the Division on our right. Firing continued — the guns of this group "standing by" by 1.45 am 2uo had 2uo almost ceased and all became quiet again. At 2.45 am enemy began firing	2uo 2uo 2uo 2uo 2uo
		3.45 am	a heavy bombardment of our support trenches and front line about A5. Retaliation was fired. No infantry attack took place and all was quiet again by 3.50 am	2uo 2uo 2uo
		10 pm	During day Enemy Artillery active on our support trenches and A8. YPRES was also shelled especially the KAAIE Salient. Weather fine.	2uo 2uo
YPRES	18-6-16	8 pm	A5. A6. A7. A8. St JEAN and POTIJZE Wood were shelled on several occasions through the day with 44mms and 4.2's. Otherwise a quiet day. Weather still cold	2uo 2uo
YPRES	19-6-16	9 pm	B10. B12. lightly shelled in morning and afternoon. Also POTIJZE WOOD. Very quiet day generally. Weather cold.	2uo
YPRES	20-6-16	9 pm	A4. A6. A7. A8. and support lines shelled intermittently throughout the day, during evening B10. B11. B12 and St JEAN also shelled. We replied by firing retaliation Y at 8.40 pm. After 9 pm practically no further Artillery activity. Weather cold.	2uo 2uo 2uo

T2134. Wt. W708—776. 500000. 4/15. Sir J. C. & S.

WAR DIARY
or
INTELLIGENCE SUMMARY
(Erase heading not required.)

Army Form C. 2118

Place	Date	Hour	Summary of Events and Information	Remarks and references to Appendices
YPRES	21.6.16	11 a.m.	Enemy artillery active on our front line A6 B7.A8. B9. also communication trenches. We fired retaliation	quo
		4 p.m.	in reply. Some aerial activity	quo
		7 p.m.	Very little enemy artillery during afternoon. A few shell into KAAIE. Weather fine and warm.	quo
YPRES	22.6.16	6 p.m.	Front line, 4 communication trenches shelled intermittently throughout the day. Our batteries registered some	quo
			points on enemy front line. YPRES and KAAIE shelled. A fairly quiet day in breathen time. Two 6" How	quo
YPRES	23.6.16	9 a.m.	How joined left group at 11.30 p.m. much aerial activity throughout the day.	quo
			Front line B10. B11. A8 A6. and communication trenches lightly shelled during day. Kaaie Salient heavily	quo
			Shelled for 10 minutes at 3 p.m. also DEAD END. Two attached 6" How. Batteries registered	quo
			points on Salient C29a (Sheet 28) central. Much aerial activity throughout the day. Weather muggy, showery	quo
YPRES	24.6.16	9.15 a.m.	From 9.15am onwards. Wire cutting was carried out at C29.d.4.b. (Sheet 28) by C/90 and	quo
			on parapet and wire about C29a. 6.6.4.B/93. He 2" Trench mortars co-operated. At former target a good line	quo
			was cut and parapet much knocked about. At C29a.6.b. a patch of 30 yds was cut and enemy parapet	quo
			was greatly damaged on a front of 100 yds. Enemy retaliation was heavy on A17 A/8 also on B9 B10	quo
			and Congreve walk. Ypres was also shelled during morning.	quo
		8 p.m.	A/93 & B/93 bombarded the MOUND I5b.3.7.6½. - result very effective - the whole outline of the MOUND	quo
			appeared completely altered. Enemy retaliated on our front line with 4.2 cm & 5.9 cm air-bursts.	quo
		10 p.m.to 10.50 p.m. 11.10 p.m. and 11.20 a.m. (night 24/25th)	Also B/90 C/90 A/93 & B/93 each fired 3 rounds gunfire	quo
		11.10 a.m.	on Roads & tracks behind enemy's lines. Weather showery during morning but cleared in	quo
			afternoon	quo

Army Form C. 2118

WAR DIARY
or
INTELLIGENCE SUMMARY
(Erase heading not required.)

Instructions regarding War Diaries and Intelligence Summaries are contained in F. S. Regs., Part II. and the Staff Manual respectively. Title Pages will be prepared in manuscript.

Place	Date	Hour	Summary of Events and Information	Remarks and references to Appendices
YPRES	25.6.16	8 pm	During morning Bl90 29guns Carried out wire cutting & breaching enemy parapet on S. face of Salient C19 central. The 2" Trench mortars co-operated. Wire reported well cut in 3 places. One gun went out of action half-way thro' the firing — After an hour enemy discovered position & shelled it with 4.2 or 5.9 guns severely by this section of Bl93. In all 600 Shrapnel and 460 H.E. were fired. Enemy retaliated fairly strongly on front trench at CONTREVE WORK.	2/10 2/10 2/10 2/10 2/10
		1 pm to 6.30 pm	Preliminary bombardment of Salient carried out by all batteries of group also AB1 +B/91 attacked from Right Group and two Howitzer Batteries (4.5") from 6th Division (84, 4 D/38). The Heavy Artillery co-operated. The hour of Zero for Infantry Raiding party was fixed for 10 pm.	2/10 2/10 2/10 2/10 2/10
		10 pm	Intense bombardment was carried out according to programme, but barrage had to be kept up to 11.10 pm. The enemy used coloured rockets, double red, and green star red, in earlier part of bombardment. Enemy artillery barrage was severe on our front trenches, CAMBRIDGE Rd, HAYMARKET and X lines, and much less than usual back towards YPRES and Canal.	2/10 2/10 2/10 2/10 2/10 2/10
		11.10	Order was given to cease fire at 11.10 pm. The 84th Bty +B/38 Bde went out of action & pulled out at about 1.30 am. Weather hot & occasional showers.	2/10 4/10
YPRES	26.6.16	9.30 pm	During morning a bombardment of Enemy trenches C19 a 5.6 to C23 c 3.0 & support & communication trenches was carried out by D/93 D/90 A/93 C/90 B/93 A/90 B/90. The heavy Artillery co-operated. Effect appeared to be good. Enemy retaliation was heavy on front & support line also POTIJZE wood.	2/10 2/10 2/10
		6.18 pm	The enemy began a very heavy bombardment of our front & support line also communication trenches and ST JEAN with 4.4 mms 4.2 cms and 5.9". This continued to about 1.30 pm.	2/10 2/10

WAR DIARY or INTELLIGENCE SUMMARY

Army Form C. 2118

Place	Date	Hour	Summary of Events and Information	Remarks and references to Appendices
YPRES	26-6-16	(contd)	when bombardment slackened & died down by 8 pm. Our Heavy Artillery were called upon to do counter battery work and His group fired retaliation X at 6.45 pm and retaliation Y at 7.20 pm. All quiet by 8.30 pm. Weather - fine & hot during day - showery in evening.	
YPRES	27-6-16	2am to 4am	18 pdr Batteries fired 100 Rds on roads and tracks behind enemy lines.	
		9 AM	At about 9am B/93 began bombarding enemy front parapet at C19.4.6 & widening Lance Cul Hro' enemy wire in front of this point (See 24th Summary). B/93 fired 900 rds Shrapnel and 200 HE. C/90 also carried out similar bombardment at C29d.5.4. Both shoots very satisfactory - enemy parapet being badly breached & lane thro' wire considerably widened. The 2" Trench Mortars combined Lieut I.F. Soudamore of C/90 was wounded at his battery position during the morning. Enemy retaliation for above bombardment was prompt & strong on B/74 A/9 for half an hour, afterwards it was intermittent. The "X" line POTIJZE village and	
		3 pm	St JEAN were also shelled as well as following communication trenches GARDEN St, JOHN St, HAYMARKET.	
		9 pm	Afternoon & evening quiet. The Roads, dumps & tracks behind enemy lines were shelled 4 times at intervals during the night by 18 pdr Batteries. Weather showery	
YPRES	28-6-16	6 pm.	Generally quiet on our front. A/93 lent to RIGHT GROUP for bombardment of FREZENBERG CROSS Rds. In comparison with two previous days decline in enemy Artillery activity very marked. POTIJZE WOOD & LA BRIQUE each received a light shelling	

Army Form C. 2118

WAR DIARY
or
INTELLIGENCE SUMMARY
(Erase heading not required.)

Instructions regarding War Diaries and Intelligence Summaries are contained in F. S. Regs., Part II. and the Staff Manual respectively. Title Pages will be prepared in manuscript.

Place	Date	Hour	Summary of Events and Information	Remarks and references to Appendices
YPRES	29-6-16	6 pm	A quiet day generally on our front. B/93 & B/90 lent to Right Group for operations against enemy salient T/2604.	940
			Enemy Artillery shelled A5, A6, A7, B9 POTIJZE WOOD & ST JEAN slightly during day. At 4.30pm enemy put about 50 "77mm" 4.2cm & 5.9cm into the BELLEWAARDEBEEK Valley, also a few into DEAD END & vicinity.	940
		10.30 pm	Enemy shelled roads round YPRES very heavily with 5.9cm & 4.2cm & 4.4mm. Also the BELLEWAARDEBEEK Valley near KANIF Salient for about an hour. Three men from D.A.C. attached to D/93 wounded. Also one man belonging to A/93. Weather changeable, some rain during the night.	940
YPRES	30-6-16	12.01am	Zero for operations by Right Group. Midnight - 1.30 am. Assault by Infy raiding parties. All quiet again by 2 am.	940
		8 am to 4 pm	Bombardment of trenches around VERLORENHOEK Rd. (C.19.d) B/90 B/93 C/90 & D/93 taking part. Appeared effective. Enemy retaliation was heavy at times on our front lines opposite bombardment. A/6, A/7, B/9 and Trenches. Communication in rear shelled at intervals during day also POTIJZE WOOD. 6 Lachrymatory shells on A.3. Weather fine.	940
		10 pm	Considerable Aerial Activity during evening.	940

J.C. Gibb Lieut. RFA
for Adjt 93rd Bde RFA
1-7-16

Army Form C. 2118

WAR DIARY
or
INTELLIGENCE SUMMARY
(Erase heading not required.)

Instructions regarding War Diaries and Intelligence Summaries are contained in F. S. Regs., Part II. and the Staff Manual respectively. Title Pages will be prepared in manuscript.

Place	Date	Hour	Summary of Events and Information	Remarks and references to Appendices
YPRES	29-6-16	5 pm	A quiet day generally on our front. A/93 & B/90 lent to Right Group for operations against enemy Salient T1 a & H. Enemy Artillery shelled A.5 A4 Ab B.9 Potijze Road & St JEAN Wood lightly during day. At 4.30 pm enemy put about 50 4.2 mm & 5.9 cm into DEAD END and vicinity into Valley of BELLEWARDEBEEK. S. of LABRIQUE, also a few 4.2 cms.	
		10.30 pm	Enemy shelled YPRES heavily with 5.9s & 4.2cms & 77mms for an hour. All quiet by 11.30 pm.	
			3 Casualties reported during the night all D.A.C. men attached to D/93. A/93 also had one casualty. Weather changeable. Some rain during the night.	
YPRES	30-6-16	Midnight	Zero hour for Operations by Right group. 1.30 am. Assault by Infantry Raiding Parties.	
		2 am	All quiet again.	
		8 pm	A quiet day on the whole, enemy shelled our area lightly during morning. Some Aerial Activity in the evening.	
		10 pm to 12 midnight	Enemy put an exceptionally heavy barrage from 10 pm onwards on roads round YPRES also on the BellWARDEBEEK Valley near KABLE Salient using 77mms 4.2 cms & 5.9 cms.	

20th Div.
XIV Corps.

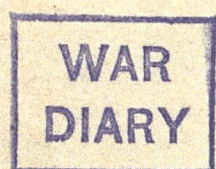

Headquarters,

93rd BRIGADE, R.F.A.

J U L Y

1 9 1 6

Army Form C. 2118

93rd Bde RFA

WAR DIARY
or
INTELLIGENCE SUMMARY
(Erase heading not required.)

Instructions regarding War Diaries and Intelligence Summaries are contained in F. S. Regs., Part II. and the Staff Manual respectively. Title Pages will be prepared in manuscript.

Place	Date	Hour	Summary of Events and Information	Remarks and references to Appendices
YPRES	1-7-16	12.15 am to 1.30 am	Enemy dumps roads & tracks behind his lines shelled with 120 rds shrapnel at odd intervals by 4.5 how. B.190 also x 8143. A quiet day generally on our front. Enemy put a few 77 mms & 2 cms into POTIZE Wood by 4 Bir. Congreve walk during day.	2uo 2uo
		5 pm	From 5.30 pm to 10 pm all Battery positions were shelled more o less heavily practically no damage done or any casualties. During the night various points behind the enemy lines roads etc were shelled by us. Weather fine.	2uo 2uo 2uo 2uo
YPRES	2-7-16	6.15pm 6.15pm	A quiet day generally. During the evening YPRES was fairly heavily shelled also Congreve walk and POTIZE Wood. During the night we fired on roads, dumps etc behind the enemy lines.	2uo 2uo 2uo
YPRES	3-7-16		Another quiet day. Enemy put a few shells into our front & support lines. Evening & night very quiet. Weather fine.	2uo 2uo
YPRES	4-7-16		Very quiet during morning. B.10 & received about a dozen 5.9 cms. during morning. In the afternoon about 200 or 300 4 mms were fired into vicinity of I.1 & 2.9. One man belonging to 4 Bir was wounded. Weather bad rain most of the day.	2uo 2uo 2uo 2uo
YPRES	5-7-16	5 pm	Quiet generally during day over front line received a few shell. Some 5.9's into garden St John Cr of B.10. At 5 pm a bombardment was carried out by the Batteries of the group on enemy John St front line about C.29.d.4.6 to C.29.d.5.4. & 4.6. Parapet & wire much knocked about. Retaliation was slow commencing but considerable when once started. A 4.1 mm barrage was placed on our front line opposite bombardment. A/6 was heavily shelled also B.9. on "S" line Haymarket John St. Weather fine	2uo 2uo 2uo 2uo 2uo 2uo 2uo 2uo

WAR DIARY or INTELLIGENCE SUMMARY

(Erase heading not required.)

Army Form C. 2118

Instructions regarding War Diaries and Intelligence Summaries are contained in F. S. Regs., Part II. and the Staff Manual respectively. Title Pages will be prepared in manuscript.

Place	Date	Hour	Summary of Events and Information	Remarks and references to Appendices
YPRES	6-7-16		A bombardment on Salient C29 central was carried out during the afternoon. Communication trenches were also shelled with Shrapnel. Effect of bombardment appeared good. A lot of timber was thrown up. Retaliation was not so heavy as usual & was mostly confined to our front line nothing heavier than a 4.2 was seen. Enemy wire was also cut at C29 d 4.5. the parapet being afterwards shelled again with H.E. Result good & at least one lane was cut. During morning our front line was lightly shelled at intervals with "M" mors. Also Garden S! Potijze Wood. Weather Good.	Geo Geo Geo Geo Geo Geo Geo
YPRES	7-7-16	1 am to 2 am	Roads, dumps & communication trenches behind enemy lines shelled at intervals by 18 p! Batteries of left group. During morning wire was again cut at C29a "4.5" and parapet behind fired on with H.E. At C29 a 8's parapet was laid open to communication French behind. At 10 am a concentrated bombardment of front trench system opposite WIELTJE was carried out. The observation on this ground is very limited but effect seemed good. Retaliation mostly on our front line at A8 & B9 & some on CONGREVE WALK. Never heavy & mostly with 44 mms & 4.2 cms. Weather changeable with heavy showers of rain. During afternoon YPRES was shelled & quiet night.	Geo Geo Geo Geo Geo Geo Geo Geo Geo Geo
YPRES	8-7-16	11 am 11:30 am to 12 noon	During morning enemy shelled B9, B.11, A5 & A6, Potijze Wood & Garden St. with a few 4" mms. At 11:30 am we bombarded THE MOUND (I5b34) with all available batteries of the group. The 2" Trench mortars co-operated. Effect appeared good on all the trenches that could be observed. The N.W. corner was quite destroyed and the front breached all along. All wire in front of THE MOUND has also disappeared. Enemy retaliation was not heavy. "M" mms, 7.h.2 cms mostly on front line. It ceased abruptly as soon as our	Geo Geo Gee Geo Geo

1875 Wt. W593/826 1,000,000 4/15 J.B.C. & A. A.D.S.S./Forms/C. 2118.

Army Form C. 2118.

WAR DIARY
or
INTELLIGENCE SUMMARY
(Erase heading not required.)

Place	Date	Hour	Summary of Events and Information	Remarks and references to Appendices
YPRES.	8-7-16 (cont)		fired ceased. Some of this retaliation was in enflade from direction of PILKEM RIDGE. During afternoon the X line in I 4 d & I 10 b was shelled with 4.2 cms. Weather changeable.	40 40
YPRES.	9-7-16	1 am to 7 am	Roads, tracks, dumps &c behind enemy's line were subjected to bursts of fire by all 18 pdr Batteries of the Group. From 7 am to 2 pm the N.E. bend of YPRES was heavily shelled with 5.9cms, 4.2cms, 4.1mm & 10mm. A quantity of lachrymatory shell being used. At 3 pm he bombarded the FREZENBERG REDOUBT. Dugouts being burnt to group of this operation, result on redoubt appeared to be fairly good. With 12 pdrs a supposed O.P. at C.30.d.4.9. was destroyed, parapet of trench was breached. Most damage was done from D.25.c.1.4 to C.30.d.9.9. There was practically no enemy retaliation on our front line trenches, enemy evidently taking our bombardment as retaliation for his bombardment of YPRES. A quiet night. Weather fine.	20 20 20 20 20 20 20 20 20 20
YPRES.	10-7-16	from about 6.45 am to 2 pm	enemy bombarded N end of YPRES heavily, majority of shell falling in vicinity of DEAD END and SALVATION CORNER (I.1.d.o.7) Calibre of shell various.	
YPRES.	" "	to 30 pm	All Batteries of the Bde took part in bombardment during first nine hours IS.6.9.2. to C.29.a.3.9 (two Batteries of the 90 & 91 & Bdes also assisted) accompanied by a discharge of gas and smoke which lasted for 30 minutes from our trenches opposite VERLORENHOEK and also ammunition bottles in front of WIELTJE Under cover of and immediately following this discharge the 5 Infy Bde made & dealt in force raiding enemy's front line at the furnace place & one at the CATTZ, opposite VERLORENHOEK one party only reached the objective namely THE MOUND and returned	

[signature]

WAR DIARY
or
INTELLIGENCE SUMMARY

Army Form C. 2118

Place	Date	Hour	Summary of Events and Information	Remarks and references to Appendices
YPRES	16.7.16	10.30 p.m.	Without Casualties. The other three parties from the enemy scanning his parapet. Strongly and so returned. The party opposite WIELTJE reached enemy wire & sat on without opposition from immediate front, but on approaching the parapet found it strongly manned and were subjected to heavy rifle and bombing at close range. They returned with several casualties. Two R.E. discharged by the lot? as on enemy by some seven seven minutes before Zero hour, and the enemy was therefore prepared & had fires lit in his parapet & his sentry who SOS rockets before the Zero hour. We do not seem to have much effect. Potshots through similar in army thrown several hours after in early heavy gasp on one flanks of the front line, at one taken up in succession from night to left or after also the fire on parapet. Enemy also Caused almost immediately in succession of fire line & the remainder of the night passed quietly.	[signature]
YPRES	11·7·16	12.30a.m. midday	All quiet again. Enemy shelled our front line intermittently during day also Garden St. X8. Potijze Wood. At 3.20 pm enemy put some French mortars into B.9. We replied firing retaliation Z. about 120 rds, at 3.50 pm & again at 5.20 pm. Enemy then shelled B11 B12 4 X8 heavily with 4·2 cms & 4" mins between 5.30 pm & 6.40 pm. A quiet night on the whole	200 200 200 200
	7 pm.		with nothing else to report. Weather fine	

WAR DIARY or INTELLIGENCE SUMMARY

Army Form C. 2118

Place	Date	Hour	Summary of Events and Information	Remarks and references to Appendices
YPRES	12-7-16		During day enemy shelled Bq B10 B11 X line A7 & A8 intermittently with 77mm & 4.2cm. We fired retaliation Z in reply to enemy shelling of Bq & B10 at 9.45 a.m. During afternoon we fired at two or three hostile batteries at intervals.	B10 B10 B10
		6 p.m.	Enemy began a very heavy bombardment of our front line trenches A6 to B10 & communication trenches, we fired Retaliations W. X. Y. and also 5 rds per gun on night lines, all quiet again by 7.30 p.m. Night passed quietly. Weather fine.	B10 B10 B10 B10
YPRES	13-7-16		During day enemy shelled A6 A8. B12. X line & garden St at intervals with 77mm. At 8.50 p.m. & 10.10 p.m. enemy shelled A6. By & Garden St with a few 77mm & 4.2cm. At request of Infantry Brigadier our guns did practically no shooting. Weather fine.	B10 B10 B10 B10
YPRES	14-7-16	5 p.m.	During morning enemy put some 44mm & 4.2cm into A7. A6. B11 & Potijze Wood also Garden St. Our guns did no shooting. A quiet night. Day fine	B10 B10
YPRES	15-7-16	6 p.m.	Generally quiet during morning. During afternoon A/30 cut wire at E.23.d.9.9. and breaching parapet behind. Wire cutting very satisfactory a lane of 50 yds being cut clean. Fuze 80 was used & burst regularly. HE on parapet effect poor. D/93 (Howitzer) afterwards fired 150 Rds on same parapet & trenches being made. Enemy retaliation practically nil. Cutting at I.5.b.5.4. Result satisfactory. Wire destroyed.	B10 B10 B10 B10 B10 B10 B10
	17-7-16	4 p.m.	A fairly quiet day. During morning a section of B/90 carried out wire	B10
	17-7-16	4 p.m.	A quiet day. Enemy Bq. shelled Bq. B10 B11 during day. When we retaliated B/B, & April Thomas	B10

Army Form C. 2118

WAR DIARY
or
INTELLIGENCE SUMMARY
(Erase heading not required.)

Place	Date	Hour	Summary of Events and Information	Remarks and references to Appendices
YPRES	18.7.16	9am	Lt. Col. A. MELLOR 90" Bde: assumed Command of "Left Group. 93" Bde R.F.A. 2nd Qr. handed over to 90" Bde R.F.A 2nd Qr. and proceeded to rest-billets at WATOU All positions of 93rd Bde render separate Diaries & detailed arm's from this date	Attd

J. H. Denman
Capt. for O.C.
ADJUTANT 93rd BRIGADE R.F.A.

31-7-16.

93rd Bde. R.F.A.
20th Div.

WAR DIARY

"D" BATTERY.

JULY
(17.7.16-31.7.16)
1916

Army Form C. 2118.

D/93 Bty RFA
(until left group)

WAR DIARY
or
INTELLIGENCE SUMMARY.
(Erase heading not required.)

Instructions regarding War Diaries and Intelligence Summaries are contained in F.S. Regs., Part II. and the Staff Manual respectively. Title pages will be prepared in manuscript.

Place	Date 1916	Hour	Summary of Events and Information	Remarks and references to Appendices
Ypres.	17 July		Nil.	
"	18 "		Nil.	
"	19 "	3.30 pm	Fired 200 H.E. on front trench in Salient. C.29.a. as per programme.	
"	20 "		Nothing to report.	
"	21 "	9 am	No 1 of Forward gun in St Jean wounded at duty.	
"	"	12 m-16.13o am	Fired 320 H.E. on Support trench extending over C.29.a & 6	
"	22 "		Nil.	
"	23 "	8.30 am	Fired 130 H.E. at request of Infantry on front trench C.33.c in retaliation	
"	"	11.45 am	1 N.C.O + 5 gunners of Forward gun in St Jean wounded by prematures of guns. (100 fuze.) 3 drivers transferred to Battery as re-inforcement from + section D.T.R.C. 1 driver at Wagon Line kicked by horse sent to hospital.	
"	24 "	9 pm	Fired 11 H.E. on trench C.29.a.s.l. supports trench behind at request of Infantry on supposed position of minenwerfer firing on B 9.	
"	25 "	4.15 – 5 pm	Fired 22 H.E. on Jasper farm + Queen" trench C.29.a.8.4. – C.29.c.2.7. at request of Infantry in retaliation for shelling of road barrier. Four gunners from No 1 Sec. D.T.R.C. transferred to Battery as re-inforcement	
"	30 "	7 pm	Fired 6 H.E. on trench D.20.c. at request of Infantry	

1577 Wt.W.10791/1773 500,000 1/15 D.D.&L. A.D.S.S./Forms/C. 2118.

Army Form C. 2118.

WAR DIARY
or
INTELLIGENCE SUMMARY.
(Erase heading not required.)

Instructions regarding War Diaries and Intelligence Summaries are contained in F.S. Regs., Part II. and the Staff Manual respectively. Title pages will be prepared in manuscript.

Place	Date 1916.	Hour	Summary of Events and Information	Remarks and references to Appendices
Ypres.	26 July		NIL.	
	27 "	2.15am	D.20.b.1.9 & D.21.a.3.5 registered. 3 direct hits	
		6.30am	Fired 21 H.E. on front trench — Retaliation at request of Infantry.	
	28 "	noon	Fired 12 H.E. on Bevicote road.	
		1 p.m.	Fired 18 H.E. on front trench at request of Infantry.	
	29 "	10.30am	Fired 41 H.E. on road near Windmill & farms & Xrds on St. Julien.	
	30 "	7pm	Fired 1 H.E. at transport on road D.20.c.	
	31 "	6pm	Fired 25 H.E. on Langleydhall, 12 direct hits, farm burnt to the ground.	
		7pm	Fired 25 H.E. on Windmill Cottage.	
		7.30am	Fired 7 H.E. on Low Farm. 2 direct hits.	

93rd Bde. R.F.A.
20th Div.

WAR DIARY

"A" BATTERY.

JULY

(7.7.16 to 31.7.16)

1916

WAR DIARY
or
INTELLIGENCE SUMMARY.
(Erase heading not required.)

Army Form C. 2118.

A/93 Bty RFA
(with "Left" Group)

Place	Date	Hour	Summary of Events and Information	Remarks and references to Appendices
YPRES	17.7.16	9.0 a.m.	A/93 Battery became a detached unit during the 93rd Bde Hdqrs going back to rest at WATOU and Lt. Col. Mellor D.S.O. and 90th Bde Hdqrs taking over. Command of LEFT GROUP. Infantry supported by Battery were 11th ESSEX Regt. of 6th Div. and the right company of Left Batts. of 6th Div.	ref
		5.0 p.m.	Battery fired 20 rounds of J.A. and 47 rounds of J.A.X. at FREZENBURG REDOUBT and houses to South.	ref
"	18.7.16		Quiet morning and nothing to record – Battery morning shifting & working parts.	ref
		4 p.m.	Battery shelled FREZENBURG REDOUBT and houses to South, firing during day 15 A and 35 A.X.	
	19.7.16		Quiet morning and nothing to record.	ref
		4.0 p.m.	Battery bombarded front trenches just north of VERLORENHOEK Road. Much damage was done to parapet – one large breach was made and several craters – Ammunition fired was 57 A.X. Enemy firing no casualties.	
	20.7.16		During morning nothing to record.	ref
		10.10 p.m.	Began to cut wire just South of MOUND – fired 187 A. – Observation almost impossible & heavy mist causing short bursts till 2.0 a.m. 21st – Results were uncertain Flare was at first expected – Parapet much damaged and a good deal of wire cut.	
	21.7.16		Very quiet day. Battery fired 95 A and 62 A.X. at Gun pits by IBERIAN FARM and were testing S.O.S. lines etc.	ref

1577 Wt. W10791/1773 50,000 1/15 D. D. & L. A.D.S.S./Forms/C. 2118.

WAR DIARY or INTELLIGENCE SUMMARY

Army Form C. 2118.

Instructions regarding War Diaries and Intelligence Summaries are contained in F. S. Regs., Part II. and the Staff Manual respectively. Title pages will be prepared in manuscript.

(Erase heading not required.)

Place	Date	Hour	Summary of Events and Information	Remarks and references to Appendices
YPRES	22.7.16.		Very quiet morning and that was nothing to record. In afternoon enemy fired 100 A+ at STATION BUILDINGS etc - many direct hits obtained.	Ref. C.
	23.7.16.		Nothing to report in morning. Quiet day. Bty. fired 8A+40At in regulation etc.	Ref. Q.
	24.7.16.	11.57pm	Some firing on left and report of gas alarms being heard, but nothing happened. Quiet day and nothing to report. Bty. fired 20 A+ in registration etc.	Ref. J.
	25.7.16.		Very quiet day and little shooting on either side. During day the Bty. fired 41A+32AX in registration and har. fire in VERLORENHOEK.	Ref. C.
	26.7.16.	9.45pm.	A minor enemy attack developed on the Salient - held a form to be at ST. ELOI.	
		5.35pm.	Quiet morning and nothing to record. Enemy shelled HAY MARKET and Bty. fired 30A+ in retaliation. Bty. also fired 80A+ 20 A+ at Hannix evening bathes.	Ref. P.
	27.7.16.		A quiet normal day and nothing to record. Bty fired 13A+ 48A+ at shelled and fortified houses etc.	Ref. P.
	28.7.16.	1.0pm. 2.0pm.	Bty. fired 11A+ 12AX at VERLORENHOEK. Hostile Bty. was located at 5x5d 3i X1 and engaged by 60 rdrs. This Bty. was active in shelling YPRES.	Ref. P

WAR DIARY or INTELLIGENCE SUMMARY

Army Form C. 2118.

Place	Date	Hour	Summary of Events and Information	Remarks and references to Appendices
YPRES	29.7.16		Very quiet morning and nothing to record. During morning visited the S.O.S. lines. Bty. fired 13A + 15 AX. 2/Lt. E.M. Fawell who had been attached to Bty. was posted to Btc. and joined next section.	
	30.7.16		Bty. together with rest of 10th Div. Arty. became attached to 29th Division, as 50th Div. has Div. Arty. have gone South to neighbourhood of Somme. Bty. fired 6A + 8AX in finding no connector and registration.	meP
	31.7.16		Very quiet day and nothing to record. Bty. fired 17 AX on dugout by FREZENBURG + Rds.	meP

McClary Capt. RFA.
Comdg A/93 RFA.

20Th Divisional Artillery.

BATTERY DIARIES ATTACHED

93rd BRIGADE R. F. A.

AUGUST 1 9 1 6

Y/13

Confidential.

War Diary
of
93rd Bde R.F.A.

From 1-8-16
To 31-8-16

(VOLUME) XIV

WAR DIARY
or
INTELLIGENCE SUMMARY

93rd Bde R F A Army Form C. 2118

Map references from 1st Col Müller 20.8.16 "Left Corps" from 1st Col Müller 20.8.16

Posn to 22/8/16 Batteries with 6th Inf Bde - vide attached sheet

Place	Date	Hour	Summary of Events and Information	Remarks and references to Appendices
YPRES	22.8.16	5.30pm	Lt Col A & D Nos. 93rd Bde RFA hr rec'd Command of left Group from Lt Col Müller 20.8.16	Pyrs
		6am	Weather fine. About 12 rifle grenades fired into our front line about WIELTJE to which 75/90 batty retaliated briskly.	
		9pm.	Weather fine a quiet day with occasional shelling of our front line & Comm' trenches about WIELTJE turner. We retaliated briskly. Hostile airoplane activity by hostile aides.	Pyrs
"	24.8.16	8pm	Weather fine a quiet day with practically no enemy A/c activity. Some aerial activity by hostile airmen.	Pyrs
	25.8.16	9pm	Very quiet generally on our front. Weather hot & muggy a little rain during evening much aerial activity during the day.	Euo.
	26.8.16	9pm.	Very quiet during day. At 8pm a small bombardment on enemy's front trenches. N. of point C29d54 was carried out. The 2" Trench mortars of D.93. fired on front trenches. C/90 B/90, B/93 & D/90 also took part. A high following wind made accurate shooting difficult. TM's claimed 10 direct hits on front parapet. Wire in front of parapet & parapet itself damaged. Damage on 2nd line probably considerable, much timber being thrown up. Enemy retaliation was slight. Enfilade 4.9cm battery on A4 & A8. 8.6cm on Cambridge Rd. 4.2cm on Warwick F.M. No damage done. Weather fair.	Suc.
	27.8.16	9pm	Weather unsettled a quiet day on front line except Enn's Trenches were highly shelled to which we retaliated. Otherwise no feature of interest	Pyrs.
	28.8.16	9pm	Weather fine a very quiet day batty quiet	Pyrs.

Army Form C. 2118

WAR DIARY
or
INTELLIGENCE SUMMARY
(Erase heading not required.)

Instructions regarding War Diaries and Intelligence Summaries are contained in F. S. Regs., Part II. and the Staff Manual respectively. Title Pages will be prepared in manuscript.

Place	Date	Hour	Summary of Events and Information	Remarks and references to Appendices
YPRES	29.8.16	9 p.m.	A quiet day generally. Enemy shelled Potijze Wood with 10.5 cm that & 10.11 from 8.6 mm & 4.4 mm guns into St Jean & Garden St. At about 9.40 p.m. Gas Alarm sounded	See See See
		11 p.m.	on our right, all Batteries "stood-to". Infantry reported all quiet on our front. Broke off at 11.30 pm. Weather fine.	See See
	30.8.16	9 p.m.	Rained hard all day. During day enemy put a few 10.5 cm. 4.4m into A8. B9. & B10. we fired (DH3) 10 rds in retaliation. Otherwise no feature of interest.	See See
	31.8.16	4 p.m.	Enemy put a few 10 cm H.V. gun shells into DEAD END & YPRES during morning. Nothing else to report. Weather fine.	See See

S. L. O'B. Dyke
Lt. R.F.A.
Orderly Officer. 93rd Bde. R.F.A.

A/93 Battery F.2118
Army Form C. 2118.

WAR DIARY
or
INTELLIGENCE SUMMARY
(Erase heading not required.)

Place	Date	Hour	Summary of Events and Information	Remarks and references to Appendices
YPRES.	1.8.16.		Battery together with rest of 20th Div. Arty. became attached to 29th Division. Ka Infantry of which Battery is to cover. Quiet day and nothing to record. Battery fires 13 shrapnel and 18 HE at dugout at Frezenburg and also at machine gun in front line.	Map Reference to Sheet 28
	2.8.16.		Quiet day except for little shelling of YPRES. Battery fired 90 shrapnel at VERLOREN HOEK and 4.2 Bty. behind FREZENBURG.	Ref.
	3.8.16.		During morning a few 5.9's on A8 + A9. Infantry in front line 18th Batn. KOSB. Quiet day. Bty. fires 46 shrapnel searching VERLOREN HOEK	Ref.
		10. p.m.	Heavy firing onright towards RAILWAY WOOD.	Ref.
	4.8.16.		Nothing to record. Bty. fired 39 A + 41 AX at horses.	Ref.
	5.8.16.	9.a.m.	C/90 & 319/ heavily shelled by h.v. Bty. w. 2 Bty. from behind FREZENBURG Crest. A/93 fires at stn. Bty. which stopped firing. Battery fires 54 shrapnel and 32 HE at BULL COTTAGE, above to 2 Aly ad MOUND.	Ref.
	6.8.16.		Quiet day except for few shell in square d.4 YPRES. Bty. fires 6 shrapnel a 74 HE at 4.2 Bty. BULL COTTAGE + HOGS COTTAGE. The whole firing Turned down by firat round.	Ref.

WAR DIARY
or
INTELLIGENCE SUMMARY

Army Form C. 2118.

Place	Date	Hour	Summary of Events and Information	Remarks and references to Appendices
YPRES.	7.3.16.		Very Quiet Day. Bty fires 49 shrapnel and 111 HE at 4.2 Bty STATION BUILDING sh—	ref
	8.3.16	10am	Quiet Day. Gas alarm-wore gas helmets for one hour. Bty allots C35 D.A.15Bn as fires 135 HE and 57 shrapnel on enemy trench — Bty — enemy fires 12 minenwerfer shells — aeroplane fires one round on IST.5.4. Very successful attack by municipals & Hants suffered heavy casualties.	ref
	9.3.16		Quiet Day. Battery fires 11 HE + 57 shrap. at enemy and aeroplane registration 150 rounds killing relieved by Royal Fusiliers.	ref
	10.3.16	9.30pm	Quieter day. Bty 12 HE + 52 shrap in retaliation for raid.	ref
	11.3.16		Very Quiet Day. Bty fires 95 HE + 8 shrap at BILL COTTAGE.	ref
	12.3.16	3.am	Heavy bombardment on enemy — MOUNT SORREL Bty fires 45 HE + shrap. at TRENBURG dug.	ref
	13.3.16		Very Quiet Day. Bty fires 5 shrap.	ref

WAR DIARY
or
INTELLIGENCE SUMMARY.
(Erase heading not required.)

Army Form C. 2118.

Place	Date	Hour	Summary of Events and Information	Remarks and references to Appendices
YPRES	14.3.16		Fairly quiet day. Rly. lines 3 Shrap. 4/16 HE at IBERIAN FMS & in retaliation hostile aeroplane over Rly. at night.	ueP.
	15.3.16		Quiet day. Rly fires 7 Shrap + 115 HE at St. RLY + COW HOUSE	ueP.
	16.3.16		Fairly quiet. Enemy 70 HE at FREZENBURG REDOUBT.	ueP.
	17.3.16		Quiet day. Enemy 30 HE. retaliation.	ueP.
	18.3.16		Very Quiet. Rly fires 15 HE + 75 Shrap. at St 2 RLY + SEXTON HOUSE Very quiet - Rly. fires 9 HE.	ueP.
	19.3.16		Very quiet - Rly. fires 9 HE.	ueP.
	20.3.16		Quiet day except that BP (NEW GOD) was "shelled with high velocity gun - 7 near hits - 7 near hits. My gun has been alive HE + shrap - no damage to detachment. Eng 30 HE + 31 Shrap.	ueP.
	21.3.16		Bombardment on salient 6.19 by Germans & T.M's to blowing gas cylinders - BS fired shrap on front line - Enemy 3 HE at St. RLY Enemy. Gas alarm at 6.15 pm till 4.05 pm.	ueP.
	22.3.16		Very quiet. Eng 20 Shrap.	ueP.

Period 23/3 to 31/3 see 93' Bde. Diary

McGary Capt RFA
Comd. A/93 RFA

B/93 Battery

Army Form C 2118

WAR DIARY
or
INTELLIGENCE SUMMARY.
(Erase heading not required.)

Instructions regarding War Diaries and Intelligence Summaries are contained in F.S. Regs., Part II. and the Staff Manual respectively. Title pages will be prepared in manuscript.

Place	Date	Hour	Summary of Events and Information	Remarks and references to Appendices
YPRES	1/6/16	10 P.M.	Map reference to Sheet 28. Very hot day with little artillery action. Much aeroplane activity. Some registration by aeroplane. All officers of battery went over and altered air position O.C. went out to gun lines and found the horses in very good condition.	W.T.S.A
	2/6/16	10 P.M.	Quiet day. Not much firing. Many aeroplanes out. Aeroplane fight down in No-Man's Land but not normally dangerous.	W.T.S.A
	3/6/16	10 P.M.	All day quiet. Artillery not very active. Fired several times on enemy trench mortars retaliating on enemy trenches.	W.T.S.A
	4/6/16	10 P.M.	Enemy artillery more active. Battery had to fire several retaliations for enemy trench mortars & many 15in high-velocity guns.	W.T.S.A
	5/6/16	10 P.M.	Fairly quiet day, but enemy firing now seem sound in Ypres and Valley Dressing & went to Poon.	W.T.S.A

1577 Wt. W10791/1773 50,000 1/15 D.D.&L. A.D.S.S./Forms/C.2118

WAR DIARY or INTELLIGENCE SUMMARY

(Erase heading not required.)

Army Form C. 2118.

Place	Date	Hour	Summary of Events and Information	Remarks and references to Appendices
	6/8/16	10 P.M.	Fairly busy day. Enemy shelled two separate times fur enemy found with trench mortars & their shifts velocity fun up till noon. In the evening two of our planes dropped incendiary and smoke bombs on fields behind Zonnebeke. Either to fire them or to attempt first crops a fire operation fallen. W.T.S.A.	
	7/8/16	10 P.M.	All day fairly quiet. Enemy firing into Ypres from early morning. Battery fired on the retaliation on enemy shelled our position. W.T.S.A.	
	8/8/16	11 P.M.	Enemy with aeroplane co-operation, shelled our battery position, working at 10 four guns and two ammunition pits. Supposed Gm attack reported at about 10.20 P.M. The men who had received doctor temporarily were all warned & being received an S.O.S. from the front left R Village fired the R.X and 2Lb Atkinson & Collins firing any the L X wit were able to fire. The four guns getting off about 300 Rds. W.T.S.A.	

Place	Date	Hour	Summary of Events and Information	Remarks and references to Appendices
	9/9/16	10 P.M	Very hot fine day. Enemy aeroplane on hostile position all day. Enemy fired at our Artillery position again to-day & put reported gun out of action. Lt. Collins is now to be attached to Major Fairs Bty. A Go with his men from our R.T. Major Fairs is to take over L+ Carr and an entire detm. up to 16 stages. This leaves us with two guns only.	N/11/3
	10/9/16		Warm fine day, misty in the morning. 2 new W.T.S. Atkinson proceeded to VII Army Artillery School. Tilques. for a course of instruction	N/11/3
	11/9/16	11 pm	Warm day with a mist. Enemy fairly quiet. Fired some retaliation in the afternoon for enemy shelling our front-line. Registered buildings in Zendrale and other places in enemys reinf. areas. One gun received from C/93 And placed temporarily in action in new emplacement on dirt road S of road at I.2.a.5.1 and manned by (subsection detachment). We have flew three guns in action	N/11/3

Army Form C. 2118.

WAR DIARY
or
INTELLIGENCE SUMMARY.
(Erase heading not required.)

Instructions regarding War Diaries and Intelligence Summaries are contained in F. S. Regs., Part II. and the Staff Manual respectively. Title pages will be prepared in manuscript.

Place	Date	Hour	Summary of Events and Information	Remarks and references to Appendices
	12/8/16	10 pm	Warm fine day. Heavy shelling heard from the South. Enemy artillery quiet throughout the day.	
	13/8/16	10 pm	Warm misty morning. Enemy artillery fairly active on left flank front during the morning. Three retaliations fired and shelling ceased. Afternoon warm and windy.	
	14/8/16	10 pm	Warm fine day. Enemy artillery fairly quiet during the day. We did practically no firing.	
	15/8/16	10 pm	Warm and fine. Enemy quiet throughout the day. We did no shooting. MBR proceeding to building of gun pits of L/F section.	
	16/8/16	10 pm	Warm fine day. Carried out small retaliations in early morning for shelling of front line. The B.C. registered the guns of the left section in their new positions during the morning. Enemy very quiet for the remainder of the day.	
	17/8/16	11 am	A Hulce Gas Alarm was given in the early hours of the morning. The Battery stood by for about an hour, nothing further occurred.	

1577   Wt.W10791/1773   50,000   1/15   D.D. & L.   A.D.S.S./Forms/C. 2118.

WAR DIARY
or
INTELLIGENCE SUMMARY.
(Erase heading not required.)

Army Form C. 2118.

Place	Date	Hour	Summary of Events and Information	Remarks and references to Appendices
	18/5/16 (cont)	10 p.m	The firing was done, hostile in the day we fired on enemy working-party on their parapet north of St Julien Road and dispersed them. Cooker and showers throughout the day. Enemy artillery more active in the late afternoon and evening. Fire are proceeding with strengthening of gun positions.	
	19/5/16	10 p.m	Cool and showery during the day. Enemy artillery fairly active during the morning. Work proceeding round gun positions	
	19/5/16	10 p.m	Rain fell steadily during the morning, finer in the afternoon. Enemy artillery quiet. Registered the five guns of the left section on their zero lines. N.W.08?	
	20/5/16	10 p.m	A quantity of rain fell during the day. Enemy artillery quiet. Work continued on gun emplacements. N.W.08	

WAR DIARY
or
INTELLIGENCE SUMMARY.

Army Form C. 2118.

Place	Date	Hour	Summary of Events and Information	Remarks and references to Appendices
	21/8/16	10 pm	Warm fine day. Strong wind blowing from the North. At 3 pm Bombardment of enemy trenches at C.29 a.3.8 to 7.5. commenced as per programme. Continued with Bursts of fire until 3.30 pm firing about 193 rounds Shrapnel, whilst trench appeared to be well on enemy trench no damage to the latter was apparent. Enemy fired slight retaliation on our front line and supports, and later in the evening fired a number of heavy minenwerfer on our front trench, for which the left Group carried out an accurate intense bombardment of Jasper Farm. Enemy's mine sweeper cased fire. About 8.30 pm a Gas alarm from the Division on the left was received. The Battery stood to, but nothing further developed.	M.M.G.

Army Form C. 2118.

WAR DIARY
or
INTELLIGENCE SUMMARY.
(Erase heading not required.)

Instructions regarding War Diaries and Intelligence Summaries are contained in F.S. Regs., Part II. and the Staff Manual respectively. Title pages will be prepared in manuscript.

Place	Date	Hour	Summary of Events and Information	Remarks and references to Appendices
	12/8/16	10 pm	Warm fine day. Enemy artillery fairly active during the afternoon. Work proceeding on positions and dug-outs. No 1 gun despatched to I.O.M. for overhauling and general repair. No 3 gun become No 1 in charge of Sgt. Smith.	
	23/8/16	10 pm	Warm fine day. Very misty throughout the afternoon and evening. A 11 (the Battery O.P.) shelled in the morning with 10 cm Howitzer, no damage done. Enemy artillery fairly quiet. No 4 gun which was damaged by shell fire on the 9th inst. having been replaced in the shops of the I.O.M. is now returned and becomes No 3 in charge of Col. Heron.	
	24/8/16		Warm fine day. Enemy artillery fairly active in the early morning.	

(For remainder part of August see 93 Bde Diary.)

A. Withead
Lieutenant
Majour 2/93rd Bde R.F.A.

D.C. B/93 B½ RFA.

Army Form C. 2118.

C/93 Battery RFA

WAR DIARY
or
INTELLIGENCE SUMMARY.
(Erase heading not required.)

Place	Date	Hour	Summary of Events and Information	Remarks and references to Appendices
YPRES	1/8/16 to 22/8/16		"C" Battery 93rd Brigade RFA — This Battery was split up having two guns & detachments attached to B/93 Battery and one gun & detachment attached to C/90 Battery & one detachment only manning two 15pdr guns in the Kair Salient. For summary of events concerning these see War Diaries of B/93 & C/90 Batteries. A.G. Elliot Capt RFA O/c C/93 Battery RFA.	

WAR DIARY or INTELLIGENCE SUMMARY

Army Form C. 2118.

D/93 Battery RFA

Place	Date	Hour	Summary of Events and Information	Remarks and references to Appendices
Ypres	Aug 1st	6.30pm	Fired 21 H.E. Retaliation X at request of Infantry.	KBS
	Aug 2nd	9.0 am	Fired 20 H.E. " " " "	KBB
		8.5 am	Fired 30 H.E. S.O.S. "A7".	KBB
		10.0 am	Fired 8 H.E. S.O.S. "A7". No. 116216 Gr. Wickinson awarded 7 days F.P. No.1 for neglect of duty. No. 16333 A/Bdr Short reduced to the ranks for neglect of duty.	KBB
	Aug 3rd	5.30pm	Fired 25 H.E. on Regenburg Cross Roads.	KBB
		5.15/5.pm	Fired 15 H.E. on transport on road near Windmill Estaminet	KBB
		9.0 pm	Fired 37 H.E. Retaliation X at request of Infantry for shelling R8 with T.M. & 77 m.m.	KBB
	Aug 4th	12.10pm	Fired 14 H.E. Retaliation Z at request of Infantry. Two guns moved to new position at I.1.T.7.5.	KBB
	Aug 5th	5.55pm	Fired 8 H.E. at JASPER FARM - Retaliation as request of Infantry.	KBB
	Aug 6th	9.30 am	Fired 5 H.E. at trenches near JASPER FARM - registering new gun position	KBB
		1.0 pm	Fired 27 H.E. at JASPER FARM - retaliation for shelling B 9 + B 10.	KBB
	Aug 7th	9.55 am	Fired 10 H.E. at C.29.b.b.o. retaliation for trench mortars on A7.	KBB
		4.10 pm	Fired 20 H.E. at C.23.c.5.2 & C.23.c.7.x registration by aeroplane.	KBB
	Aug 8th	5.30pm	Fired 13 H.E. on trenches of Mobile Bdg	KBB
		6.15 pm	Fired 13 H.E. on trenches near JASPER FARM.	
	Aug 9th	10.30pm	Fired 115 H.E. S.O.S. A6+B9. - Gas attack by enemy on front.	KBB
		2.30pm	Fired 17 H.E. on CONCRETE COTTAGE + direct hits	
		5.20pm	Fired 9 H.E. at Battery Position at C.20.a.9.9. - Battery active.	KBS
	Aug 10th	4.10pm	Fired 4 H.E. on trench mortar at C.29.a.4.8½.	KBS
		2.10pm	Fired 6 H.E. on C.29.b.0.5½ in retaliation for shelling R10	Nil

WAR DIARY or INTELLIGENCE SUMMARY

Army Form C. 2118.

(Erase heading not required.)

Instructions regarding War Diaries and Intelligence Summaries are contained in F. S. Regs., Part II. and the Staff Manual respectively. Title pages will be prepared in manuscript.

Place	Date	Hour	Summary of Events and Information	Remarks and references to Appendices
Ypres.	Aug 11th	1.10 a.m.	No. 83918 Sergt. Cosey to C.C.1 taken off Strength.	KBP
	Aug 12th	5.55/run	Fired 12 H.E. on JASPER FARM in retaliation for shelling JOHN STREET. 2 direct hits	KBP
	Aug 13th	9.0 am to 9.30 am	Fired 14 H.E. N. of Salient in retaliation for shelling B.10. Fired 37 H.E. 10 rds on new work at C.29.d.5.6. 10 rds on Trench Mortar at C.29.c.1.2.	KBP
	Aug 14th	11.55 am	+17 H.E. on parapet at C.29.a.9.3. Communication trench. One dug-out blown up. Fired 6 H.E. on Jasper Farm 4 lots on 2nd 6th & 2nd shell. retaliation for trench mortars which ceased firing.	KBP
	"		Fired 10 H.E. on D.20.C.2.1 Zero Line for advanced Forward Gun – 1 direct hit.	
	Aug 15th	7.30 am	No. 37484 Bdr. Marklew to C.C.1 taken off Strength.	KBP
	Aug 16th	7.45 am to 8.30 am	Fired 7 H.E. on working party at C.23.C.O.7½. No. 26584 Gr. Rayford transferred to "G" Battery, O.H.A. Fired 31 H.E. on JASPER FARM, C.22.a.5.9. + C.22.D.O.9 in retaliation for T.Ms firing on A.8, B.9 + B.10. Considerable material went up at C.29.a.5.9. when JASPER FARM was fired on. T.Ms firing on A.8 + B.9 ceased for about 10 minutes.	KBP
	Aug 17th		83935 Gr. Pilkington to C.C.1 taken off Strength	KBP
		7.30 am	Fired 3 H.E. at working party on parapet at C.23.C.O.7½ – rounds fell in middle of party.	
	Aug 18th	4.0 pm	Fired 9 H.E. on party working on dugout at D.20.a.9.2. – dispersed.	KBP
		9.0 am	Fired 1 H.E. at working party at C.23.O.9.2.	
		3.45/run	Fired 4 H.E. at C.29.a.9.5. Checking Zero Line.	
	Aug 19th	11.15 am	Fired 25 H.E. at 10.5 cm. Battery, rounds were effective as battery ceased firing	KBP
	Aug 20th	8.50 am	Fired 6 H.E. on working party at C.23.C.9.1½. which dispersed.	KBP
		2.0 pm	Fired 15 H.E. on T.M. firing on A.8. T.M. ceased firing	KBP

Army Form C. 2118.

WAR DIARY
or
INTELLIGENCE SUMMARY.
(Erase heading not required.)

Place	Date	Hour	Summary of Events and Information	Remarks and references to Appendices
Ypres.	Aug 21.	3pm.	Fired 145 H.E. on front trench as per programme. - Retaliation by enemy feeble.	
		6:50pm	Fired 10 H.E. on Battery east of KIPP D.20.6.0.4	
		7:5pm	Fired 6 H.E. on JASPER FARM.	
		8:0pm	Fired 44 H.E. on WILLAM FARM C.27.6.09. - Retaliation for aerial torpedoes.	
		5:56am	O.P. (A 97) had 14 direct hits from 10 cm. H.V. gun. Front of house was knocked in	Y128
	2.15.6 2:30pm		Horses again fired by same gun at A 97.	
	Aug 22nd	9:50 am	Fired 8 H.E. at working party at C.23.c.6.5	
		8:55pm	Fired 8 H.E. on C.23.c.65. at request of Infantry.	Y62P

Pierced 23/8 & 31/8 see
93rd Bde Diary

T.H.B. Hoare
2nd Lt for O.C. D/93 R.F.A.

1577 Wt. W10791/1773 500,000 1/15 D. D. & L. A.D.S.S./Forms/C. 2118.

20th Divisional Artillery.

93rd BRIGADE R. F. A.

SEPTEMBER 1 9 1 6

Vol. 14

Confidential

War Diary
93rd. B de. R.F.A.
To 30th Sept 1916
From 1st Septr 1916

Army Form C. 2118.

WAR DIARY
or
INTELLIGENCE SUMMARY.
(Erase heading not required.)

Instructions regarding War Diaries and Intelligence
Summaries are contained in F. S. Regs., Part II.
and the Staff Manual respectively. Title pages
will be prepared in manuscript.

Place	Date	Hour	Summary of Events and Information	Remarks and references to Appendices
YPRES.	Sept 1st/16	8 am	Enemy trench mortared B.10. to which we retaliated. Nothing further to record. Weather fine	2xo
		9 pm		
	Sept 2nd	9 am	Very quiet all day. No feature of interest to record. Weather fine.	2xo
		11 pm	Gas alarms sounded + Batteries opened fire putting a slow barrage on their night-lines.	2xo
		11.30 pm	Ascertained gas-alarm was false firing died down by mid-night	2xo
	Sept 3rd	2 am	4th gas-alarm sounded + Infantry Bde HQrs reported gas in front of B.q. gas-alarm false	2xo
		2ue 2.00 pm	Batteries did not open fire	2xo
		3ue 3.15 am	gas-alarms – false Batteries stood-to but did not fire	2xo
			gas-alarms – false Batteries stood-to but did not fire.	2xo
		6 pm	Very quiet day nothing to report weather fine	2xo
	Sept 4	9 pm	Quiet day. A few rounds into St Jean. O.C. 14th Bde Adjutant + Orderly Officer arrived to take over. weather fair.	2xo
	5.9.16.	7.30 am	A few 44ms on to A.9. We retaliated suitably. During day enemy shelled Bq Bde B11	2xo
		7 pm	lightly with 44mms to which we retaliated. weather bad rain all day.	2xo
YPRES.	6.9.16.	5 pm	Quiet all day. At 5 pm Col. West of 93rd Bde R.F.A. handed over command to Col. Lloyd of 14th Bde 2xo-B/93 T-D/93 Batteries relieved by Batteries of 14th Bde RFA	2xo
WATOU.	6.9.16	4 pm	Temporary HQrs of 93rd Bde opened in WATOU square weather fine	2xo
WATOU	7.9.16	4 pm	weather fine. The Bde prepared for march on the 8th	2xo
			See next page	

Army Form C. 2118.

WAR DIARY
or
INTELLIGENCE SUMMARY
(Erase heading not required.)

Instructions regarding War Diaries and Intelligence Summaries are contained in F. S. Regs., Part II. and the Staff Manual respectively. Title Pages will be prepared in manuscript.

Place	Date	Hour	Summary of Events and Information	Remarks and references to Appendices
OERTEZEELE	8/9/16	7 pm	Marched from WATOU at 9am. Arrived OERTEZEELE 2pm. Batteries marched independently. Weather fine. 12 miles	euo
MARTHES	9/9/16	4 pm	Marched from OERTEZEELE at 8am. Arrived MARTHES 4pm. Brigade march. About 14 miles weather fine	euo
Monchy-Cayeux	10/9/16	4 pm	Marched from MARTHES at 8.30am. Arrived MONCHY-CAYEUX 4pm. Brigade march. About 16 miles weather fine	euo
CONCHY-SUR-Conchy	11/9/16	7 pm	Marched from MONCHY at 8.30am arrived CONCHY 12.30pm. Brigade march. About 12 miles weather fine	euo
OUTREBOIS	12/9/16	7 pm	Marched from CONCHY at 10am arrived OUTREBOIS 1.30pm. Div'nl Arty march about 12 miles weather fine	euo
FLESSELLES	13/9/16	9 pm	Marched from OUTREBOIS at 10.45am arrived FLESSELLES 5pm. Div'nl Arty march about 18 miles weather fine	euo
BOIS-DES-TAILLES sur Somme	14/9/16	9 pm	Marched from FLESSELLES at 5.25am arrived BOIS-DES-TAILLES at 3pm. Div'nl Arty march about 24 miles weather fine. Brigade Bivouaced in valley, a few tents available.	euo euo
ditto	15/9/16	9 am	Brigade resting. Preparing guns for action - sorting stores - and general clean up after march. weather fine	euo
ditto	15/9/16	4 pm	All guns - 12 pdr of A+B batteries and 3, guns 4.5 How of D Battery ready for action. Signalling drill, gun drill etc. weather fine.	euo
ditto	14/9/16	7 pm	Gun drill, signalling etc carried out by all Batteries. 1 gun (How) of D Battery returned from I.O.M. 174 fm	euo euo
ditto	16.9.16	7 pm	Rained hard all day. In afternoon handed over some gun-stores to 92nd A.A.	euo

1875 Wt. W593/826 1,000,000 4/15. J.B.C. & A. A.D.S.S./Forms/C. 2118.

Army Form C.' 2118

WAR DIARY
or
INTELLIGENCE SUMMARY
(Erase heading not required.)

Instructions regarding War Diaries and Intelligence Summaries are contained in F.S. Regs., Part II. and the Staff Manual respectively. Title Pages will be prepared in manuscript.

Place	Date	Hour	Summary of Events and Information	Remarks and references to Appendices
~~BRAY~~ B16-des-Tailles.	19.9.16	7.30 am	Col. left with Battery Commanders proceeded to "Bois de BARNAFAY" to report to C.R.A. Guards Divn.	Guo
		2.45 pm	All Batteries of Brigade marched via BRAY, CARNOY, MEUNTAUBON - BOIS-DES-TRONES + went into action at Guillemont. Roads very bad much blocked - the whole night was spent getting guns in + dumping ammunition. Weather fine some rain	Guo Guo Guo
Guillemont	20/9/16	10.01 am to 9 pm	All day spent in preparing gun platforms - digging dugouts + settling down - guns absolutely in the open, men sleeping in shell holes, great difficulties owing to mud + bad approaches. O.P.'s reconnoitred + some wires laid. This Brigade is working as part of 16th Group under Guards Divnl Arty. Rained all afternoon + evening.	Guo Guo Guo Guo
Guillemont	21/9/16	9 pm	Weather fine. A + B Batteries cut wire at 73.b.yd. (Sheet 57c S.W.). D193 registered various points all possible labour utilized to fortify positions. Visual signalling scheme with front-line reconnoitred.	Guo Guo
Guillemont	22/9/16	9 pm	Weather fine. A.B. + D. Batteries carried out shoots at various targets. Wire cutting by A + B Batteries.	Guo Guo
Guillemont	23/9/16	9 pm	Weather fine. A + B. cut wire. D Battery cut wire. D battery bombarded his BOEUFS. Guillemont shelled at intervals throughout day (by ≠ 10 cm H.V. gun. Batteries carried out shoots during the night. 1st Col. A. MELLOR D.S.O. Commdg. 'A' Battery, posted to Command 28th (Bde) R.F.A. 6th Bde.	Guo Guo Guo
Guillemont	24/9/16	9 pm	Weather fine. A+B batteries cut wire. D battery bombarded various targets. Night shooting carried out by all Batteries. Operation Orders for Y + Z days received. Time altered at 4.15 pm.	Guo Guo
Guillemont	25/9/16	12 noon	Weather fine. F.O.O's liaison officers, Signal stations established in readiness for Infantry assault. Batteries of this Brigade Shot according to operation Orders	Guo Guo
		12.35 pm	Zero hour. Infantry assault.	Guo

WAR DIARY or INTELLIGENCE SUMMARY

Army Form C. 2118

(Erase heading not required.)

Place	Date	Hour	Summary of Events and Information	Remarks and references to Appendices
Guillemont	25/9/16	4 pm	Our Offensive carried out successfully according to programme. A slow barrage was kept up by the Batteries of this Brigade on sunken road & points about N3&6 and N28 c+d, during the night (sheet 57c s.w.). Our infantry (guards) gained all their objectives, & dug themselves in.	See see see
Guillemont	26/9/16	9 am	Slow rate of fire kept up by Batteries on N3&6 & N2&6 c+d. During morning F.O.Os were sent out to re-register new front.	see see
		6 p.m.	No counter-attached delivered by germans. Night shooting on S.O.S lines carried out by batteries at slow rate of fire. Weather fine.	see see
Guillemont	27/9/16	9 a.m	New OPs selected & ground reconnoitred. A demonstration carried out at 2.15pm to assist an attack carried out by Corps on our left. Night shooting as for 26/9/16. Weather fine.	see see see
Guillemont	28/9/16	9 p.m.	Weather fine. Brigade O.P. selected at T2 d 6.1. (sheet 57c s.w). Night shooting as before.	see
Guillemont	29/9/16	7 p.m.	Registration by Direct observation & aeroplane carried out. New zone line registration by direct observation. Weather changeable. Aeroplane registration carried out.	see see
		2 p.m.	This Brigade came under orders of Lt Col Wilson of 91st Bde forming part of left group under new grouping of Artillery fronts. New S.O.S. lines came into force. Orders for this Brigade to fire 40 rds per battery per hour on S.O.S lines, searching 100 to 200 yds, throughout the 24 hrs.	see see see see
Guillemont	30/9/16	9 am	93rd became Right group under O.C. 93rd Bde R.F.A. Forward positions for Batteries reconnoitred about T2 d central. (sheet 57c s.w.). Platforms for guns etc being prepared. Weather fine.	see see

E. L. M. B. Oyler
for Adjt L? R.F.A.
93rd Bde. R.F.A.

20th Divisional Artillery.

93rd BRIGADE R. F. A.

OCTOBER 1 9 1 6

Vol 15

Confidential

War Diary.

93rd Bde R.F.A.

To 2-10-16

From 1-10-16

Army Form C. 2118.

WAR DIARY
or
INTELLIGENCE SUMMARY.
(Erase heading not required.)

Instructions regarding War Diaries and Intelligence Summaries are contained in F. S. Regs., Part II. and the Staff Manual respectively. Title pages will be prepared in manuscript.

Place	Date	Hour	Summary of Events and Information	Remarks and references to Appendices
GUILLEMONT	1-9-16.	8 a.m.	93rd Bde HdQrs + Batteries moved to a position in T.9.d. (Sheet 57c S.W.) and came under Lt. Col. Wilson of 91st Bde as part of Left Group.	Ero Ero
T.9.d. Map 57c S.W.	2-9-16	9 p.m.	During day Batteries registered + dug themselves in. Great difficulties owing to mud + rain. Night firing on S.O.S. lines + searching hollow ground back up to Le TRANSLOY. Weather bad – rain all day + night. 20 Rds per Battery per hour fired.	Ero Ero Ero Ero
ditto	3-9-16.	9 p.m.	Batteries registered various points + carried out shoots according to orders. Every possible effort made to prepare dugouts sufficient for 1000 rds per gun. Mud state of roads very bad + digging difficult. Weather bad up to 2 p.m. when cleared somewhat.	Ero Ero Ero
GUILLEMONT	1-7-16.	9 p.m.	Preparations made for move to valley beyond GUINCHY. Night firing carried out as usual – about 20 rds per Battery per hour – Weather fine.	Ero Ero
T.9.d. Map 57c S.W.	4-9-16.	–	Bad day – Col Latham came up front moved to place in dug + huts. Staff with Trench 93 Bde Staff returned to keep effective at Bdy. Batt@B's. Enemy shelled fairly heavily – one shrapnel Ger shell had him & Capt Lee. Still men alive & remain at Dg3 Bon caught 12 men all D/93. B=-	90M 9CM
"	5 + 6	–	Wire cutting and preparing for attacks timed to take place at 7h.	9CM
"	7.	–	4.15 pm 2nd Div attacked and took RAINBOW + CLOUDY Trenches. Little opposition from men. 1.45 pm. Quiet night.	9CM
"	8-10	–	Shelling fairly heavy at all times – nothing exceptional to report. Batteries fired about 20 rounds an hour day + night apart from retaliation and other targets.	9CMR

WAR DIARY
or
INTELLIGENCE SUMMARY.

(Erase heading not required.)

Army Form C. 2118.

Place	Date	Hour	Summary of Events and Information	Remarks and references to Appendices
T.d. Sheet 57.SW	11/10/16	—	Bombardment of enemy trenches all day in preparation for attack at 12" Centroid Gun Redoubt & enemy works and trenches at 2.5 p.m. by various journals at several points but eventually came back to original line.	JCRR JCRR JCRR
— " —	12/10/16	—	Nothing exceptional - usual bombardment by all batteries on enemy works, billets etc	JCRR
"	13/14	—	Attack on enemy made at 6.35 a.m. again only moderately successful.	JCRR
"	15	—	Nothing before reporting.	JCRR
"	16/10/16	"	Since 6th Bn is supported by 6th Bn Infantry from S.P.N right of 16th Regiment on Supporting all our Bde Arty and 24th Bde Arty. Work at intee to 550 R.A	JCRR JCRR
"	17/10/16	—	Enemy works and trenches constantly kept under fire, in preparation for attack burnid & take place at 12th Nothing exceptional for report.	JCRR
"	18th	"	Infantry attacked MILD Trench at 3.10 a.m. to 1st original French - Enemy artillery very active all day - weather bad weather very bad in dead - enemy trenches shelled day & night.	JCRR JCRR
"	19. 20/22	"	On heavy shelling of enemy hick elle works day & night in preparation for infantry attack timed for 5.30 pm	JCRR
"	23/10/6	"	Attack commenced for 11.30 a.m. postponed on account of mist until 2.30 p.m. Infantry attacked and gained nearly all objectives (24th B & 8th Bde) quiet otherwise no counter attack by enemy	JCRR
"	24/10/6	"	Very quiet day probably owing to excessive rain. At 9 a.m. Lt. Col. Wilson assumed command of left Group. Lt. Col. West assumed command of WEST's Group consisting of 91st & 972nd Bde (part of left group). Weather bad.	...
"	25/10/16	"	No infantry action. # Enemy Artillery activity above normal. Weather stormy, some rain.	...

Army Form C. 2118

WAR DIARY
or
INTELLIGENCE SUMMARY.

(Erase heading not required.)

Instructions regarding War Diaries and Intelligence
Summaries are contained in F. S. Regs., Part II.
and the Staff Manual respectively. Title pages
will be prepared in manuscript.

Place	Date	Hour	Summary of Events and Information	Remarks and references to Appendices
T7d. Sheet 57c S.W.	26/9/18		Nothing unusual to report. Weather fine at intervals and considerable aerial activity. Our Batteries carried out their firing of 20 rds per battery per hour throughout 24 hrs. apart from other targets.	Ends Ends
"	27/9/18 to 30/9/18		Weather very bad during the time most operations which were to have taken place on the left of 41st Div. have been postponed. "A" Section of "A" Group was & Rein moved to the operations and also "B" How Battery of 4th Bgde i.e. "B" Bewer Lupus to an accurate emplacement in the 11" position. They also two prepared lines and suitably the 9"/2" being emplaced by the 17 & 78 operative had been roughly cancelled Leaving 45/57 & 7 57 & not moving & 51 army heavy howl and concrete from always 4 AA L.A.N. engaged in AA fire ag. hostile aircraft nearly 2A.	
30/9/18				

J. Ambrose Capt RGA
for Lt. Col. Cmdg 93rd Bgde RGA

20th Divisional Artillery.

93rd BRIGADE R. F. A.

NOVEMBER 1 9 1 6

Vol 16

Confidential

War Diary

of

93rd Brigade RFA

Nov 1st to 30th 1916

WAR DIARY
or
INTELLIGENCE SUMMARY

(Erase heading not required.)

Army Form C. 2118

Instructions regarding War Diaries and Intelligence Summaries are contained in F.S. Regs., Part II. and the Staff Manual respectively. Title Pages will be prepared in manuscript.

Place	Date	Hour	Summary of Events and Information	Remarks and references to Appendices
T.7.d.6.2	1&3/11/16	—	Group consisting of 93rd & 91st still commanded by Lt Col Lecky (93rd Bde) all guns of group are in T.7. valley between Flers and Gueudecourt. Enemy artillery quiet & if not very much more active on second day and there is mid activity and activity above normal & all days as soon as ever the light was good enough for observation. On evening of 3rd 5 pm front, assisted by two batteries of G—Bde (Ricardo group) put down a small slow barrage to cover infantry (52nd & 51st Bns 17 Div) who made an attempt to take that part of enemy MILD trench still held by enemy. Failure owing to heavy bond state of ground, enemy machine guns & the fact that enemy had filled up uncompleted part of trench with mines. Night very quiet.	J.B.C.
-do-	4/11/16	—	From 8.30 to 9 am enemy shelled around group H.Q's with light shrapnel fire — no material damage. Rest of the day fairly quiet — light wind good all day D/Q.	J.B.C.
-do-	5/11/16	—	At 11.10 am. 3 18pdr and 2 4.5 how. batteries of the group carried standing-to. 18pdr by putting up slow barrage — otherwise a quiet day. D/q. battery left work and joined Ricardo group.	J.B.C.
-do-	6/11/16	—	Quiet day on the whole. Aerial activity on both sides. Rain weather unsettled.	suo
-do-	7-11-16	—	Enemy artillery activity normal. Enemy put barrage on our front at 8.30pm & again at 11.30 pm both light, heavy barrage on our left — weather unsettled	suo
-do-	8-11-16	—	Quiet up to 10 am when Enemy artillery extremely active on our front line and especially in valley T4a. T4b. all day up to 5 pm. Spasmodic shelling all night weather unsettled	suo
-do-	9-11-16	—	Quieter day. Group H.Q. moved back to GUILLEMONT (T25 a 5.9½) Nothing unusual to report.	suo
-do-	10-11-16	?		suo
T25a5.9½	11-11-16	—	Foggy day, enemy shelling well below normal. weather fine	suo

Army Form C. 2118

WAR DIARY
or
INTELLIGENCE SUMMARY
(Erase heading not required.)

Instructions regarding War Diaries and Intelligence Summaries are contained in F. S. Regs., Part II. and the Staff Manual respectively. Title Pages will be prepared in manuscript.

Place	Date	Hour	Summary of Events and Information	Remarks and references to Appendices
T25a 59½ (Sheet 57 Sw)	12-11-16		Foggy day, enemy Artillery activity normal. Our guns carried out usual bombardments	Eno.
"	13-11-16		The same as for the 12th inst. At 5am in order to assist operations in the NORTH we fired a heavy barrage for about 20 minutes. Enemy barraged GUEUDECOURT in reply, otherwise nothing to report.	Eno. Eno. Eno.
ditto	14-11-16		Enemy Artillery activity very active in T7d & T7b valley, all day. Strong counter battery work was called for and had to be maintained all day. Weather dull & foggy.	
ditto	15-11-16		Enemy Artillery again extremely active. A/93 & B/93 positions being heavily shelled weather dull but fine. At 2pm command of group was handed over to Lt Col. Wilson (91st Bde). The 93rd Bde HQrs staff moving back to their Wagon Line. A/93 B/93 and D/93 Batteries now part of Left Group – Left Artillery of 14th Corps.	
	16-11-16		A/93 B/93 & B/93 carried out shoots according to programme. A/93 & B/93 Battery positions heavily shelled all day by guns of various calibre. Weather rain but misty.	Eno.
	17-11-16		Situation quiet on the whole. Targets for our guns same as for the 16th. Weather fine	
	18-11-16		Situation quiet nothing to report. At 9pm D/93 fired chemical shell at sunken road & into quarry in N16d. A/93 & B/93 fired shrapnel. Weather fine.	
	19-11-16 20-11-16 21-11-16		Situation quiet generally. Weather unsettled – some rain.	
	22-11-16	10pm	S.O.S. message received from group. A/93 fired 30 rds. Proved to be false alarm. Weather unsettled	
	23-11-16	2pm	Half of each Battery A/93, B/93 & D/93 relieved by 2nd Anzac Artillery, & these relieving Batteries relieved rest of 3 Batteries of 4th Division	
	24-11-16			Weather bad. Much rain

WAR DIARY
or
INTELLIGENCE SUMMARY
(Erase heading not required.)

Army Form C. 2118

Place	Date	Hour	Summary of Events and Information	Remarks and references to Appendices
T14 c 9.3. sheet 57 SW	25/11/16	2 pm	93rd Bde HdQrs moved into action near Ginchy, taking over from Lt. Col Tillney of 32nd Bde RFA. A/93 & B/93 relieved Batteries of the 4th Divn at T14 c B.2. & T9 c 5.3. respectively. Relief of these Batteries completed at 3 pm. At 2 pm Lt Col A.H.D. West assumed command of left group Artillery, the group consisting of 92nd & 93rd RFAs and 36th Battery (less Bty). Quiet day weather unsettled – rain all night.	see " " " " " "
T14 c 9.3.	26/11/16		Rain all day. Battery positions very waterlogged & much mud. Half of 36th Batty relieved by half of B/92 at 3 pm. All batteries experiencing much difficulty in getting up material to the positions owing to all approaches being quagmires. Quiet day. Enemy artillery very quiet.	see " "
ditto	27/11/16		Nothing of interest to record. B/92 completed relief of 36th Batty at 3 pm. Weather fine but foggy.	see
ditto	28/11/16		Weather fine. Very quiet all day on our front, all units hard at working improving their positions, building new gunpits – dug-outs etc. At 6.30 pm enemy put up a fairly heavy barrage on our front. At 7 pm we replied by putting up a slow barrage on our S.O.S. lines. No action followed and all quiet by 7.20 pm. Weather fine, cold & misty.	see "
ditto	29/11/16		Weather again cold & very misty making observation almost impossible. Very quiet on our front all day.	see

A. W. West Lt Col
Cmg 93 Bde R.F.A.

20th Divisional Artillery.

93rd BRIGADE R. F. A.

DECEMBER 1 9 1 6

Vol 17

Confidential

War Diary

for Period 1st to 31st Dec 1916.

of

93rd Brigade R.F.A.

E. Clyfe
Lt RFA
a/Adjt 93 Bde RFA
31/12/16

Army Form C. 2118.

WAR DIARY
or
INTELLIGENCE SUMMARY.
(Erase heading not required.)

Instructions regarding War Diaries and Intelligence Summaries are contained in F. S. Regs., Part II. and the Staff Manual respectively. Title pages will be prepared in manuscript.

Place	Date	Hour	Summary of Events and Information	Remarks and references to Appendices
T14cq4.3 Sheet 57C SW	1/11/16.	—	During day artillery activity normal - observation difficult due to mist. At 9 pm Enemy put up a very heavy barrage on our support lines for 20 minutes - we replied by opening slow rate of fire on S.O.S. lines all quiet and no infantry action followed by 9.30 pm. Weather cold misty	8uo
"	2/11/16 to 4/11/16		Weather cold misty generally. Some rain at intervals. Gun guns replied when observation was possible - also carried out shoots during day according to orders. Night firing as ordered by AA 118o" (Left Arty XV CorPs). Enemy Artillery activity normal	8uo
"	5/11/16		No failures of caliber to record. Our guns carried out shoots a various points as ordered. Night firing as usual. Enemy Artillery activity normal. weather mostly dull generally	8uo
"	6/11/16 to 8/11/16		Nothing unusual to report. Weather unsettled & changeable. Work on gun pits - shell recesses - salvage etc. carried out. Artillery activity normal.	8uo
Tine App3 Ted Dpres.	9/11/16		O.C. 44th A.S.A AFA took over command of left group from D.C. 116th A.F.A. West. Left group now consists of 97th B.A.C. AFA & 92nd B.A.C AFA. Weather misty. Observation impossible. Enemy artillery activity below normal.	8uo
"	10/11/16		Nothing to report. Weather had much rain. Night firing as ordered	8uo
"	12/11/16		Shoots carried out on points behind enemy lines - night firing as usual. Weather greatly interfering with work on gun pits - shell recesses, etc.	8uo

WAR DIARY or INTELLIGENCE SUMMARY.

Army Form C. 2118.

(Erase heading not required.)

Place	Date	Hour	Summary of Events and Information	Remarks and references to Appendices
T14c A14/93 T8d-29	14/11/16 to 23/11/16		Our guns carried out shoots daily on Trench Junctions and points behind enemy lines - night firing as ordered. Weather cold one day then the next very mild at times. Went on gun pits well received, carried out but progress slow due to difficulties of transport & weather. Enemy artillery activity normal. No features of interest to record in this period.	Ello
S.W.				Ello
				Sco
"	24/11/16		During day activity normal. Weather bad. At 10 pm an S.O.S alarm was given - enemy fired a heavy bombardment but as our guns replying eventually died down by 11 pm. No infantry action followed.	Ello
"				Sco
"				Sco
"	25/11/16		Two set bombardments by our guns carried out as ordered - enemy trench junction - CEMETERY circle and LE TRANSLOY being engaged. Enemy retaliation not heavy otherwise nothing of interest occurred. Weather changeable.	Ello
				Ello
"	26/11/16		Nothing of any interest to report. Weather changeable.	Ello
"	27/11/16		Half Batteries of the 93rd RFA relieved by half batteries of its 91st BDE in the line. Activity on both sides normal.	Ello
				Ello
MORLANCOURT	28/11/16		Relief of remaining half batteries at open time completed whole Brigade marched back to MORLANCOURT.	Ello
"	29/11/16		In rest billets at MORLANCOURT. Weather unsettled.	Ello
"	30/11/16			Ello

C E Oyler Lt Col
Comdg 93 U.B RFA

www.ingramcontent.com/pod-product-compliance
Lightning Source LLC
Chambersburg PA
CBHW081548160426
43191CB00011B/1867